Between Us

www.penguin.co.uk

BANTAM PRESS

LONDON · TORONTO · SYDNEY · AUCKLAND · JOHANNESBURG

TRANSWORLD PUBLISHERS
61–63 Uxbridge Road, London W5 5SA
www.penguin.co.uk

Transworld is part of the Penguin Random House group of companies
whose addresses can be found at global.penguinrandomhouse.com

Penguin
Random House
UK

First published in Great Britain in 2016 by Bantam Press
an imprint of Transworld Publishers

A CIP catalogue record for this book
is available from the British Library.

ISBN 9780593077689

Typeset in Visby by www.envyltd.co.uk
Printed and bound in Germany by Firmengruppe Appl

Penguin Random House is committed to a sustainable
future for our business, our readers and our planet. This book
is made from Forest Stewardship Council® certified paper.

MIX
Paper from
responsible sources
FSC® C018179

1 3 5 7 9 10 8 6 4 2

I dedicate this book to my incredible family and you,
my wonderful fans, who continue to support me. I hope that you
will love reading this book in which I share many unforgettable
memories, both good and bad, with you.

This is not an autobiography, it's about special moments of my life.
Between us, it's a beaut. Enjoy.

Love,

Pete

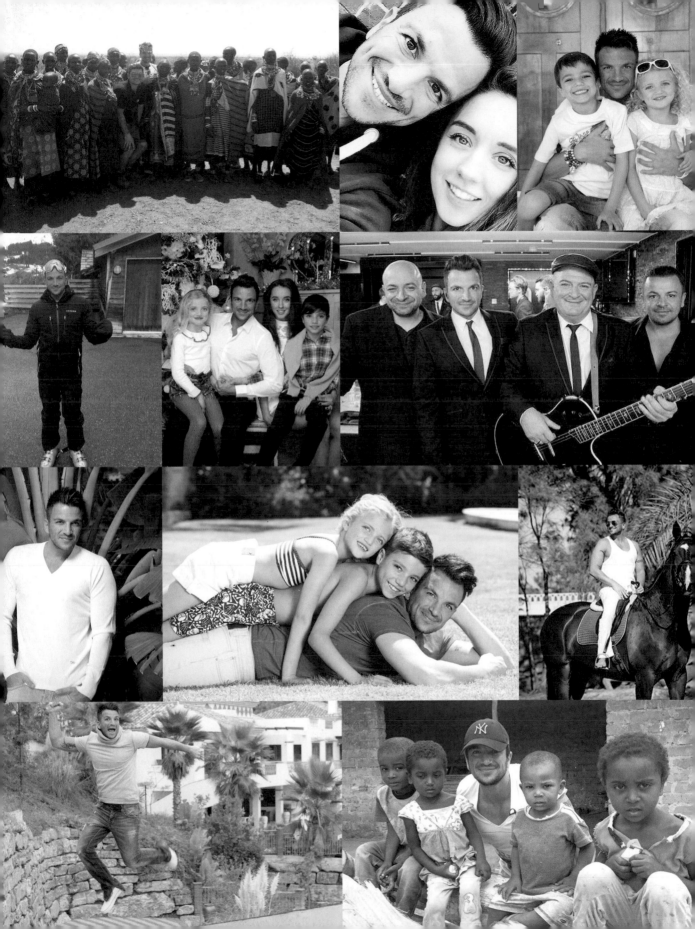

Contents

The Show
Must Go On

'I was in a hospital room. I didn't know where it was. I didn't know what time it was. All I knew was that I was in a massive amount of pain.'

The Show Must Go On

The story of my new life starts a long way from home, in Los Angeles, California. So let me tell you about LA.

For me, LA is all about inspiration. I wouldn't want to be there all the time, but when it comes to music, and creativity, it's pretty much the only place for me.

I guess it makes some kind of sense. The music I loved to listen to when I was growing up was all American. Think Motown. Think James Brown and Prince. Think Babyface and After 7 – a group that few people in the UK will have heard of, but which had a huge influence on me as a kid. Especially, think the Jackson 5, and the high points of Michael Jackson's solo career – *Thriller*, *Bad*, *Off the Wall*. All the artists that I loved had worked in LA and it's impossible to walk down Sunset Boulevard or Santa Monica Drive, soaking up the sun and taking in all the sights, and not think: wow, this is what I was dreaming about back in the day.

And now imagine what it's like to head to LA and walk straight into the studios where these amazing albums, music that had such a formative influence on me, were recorded. Imagine finding yourself, as I have done, in a studio in West Hollywood, built especially for Michael Jackson when he was recording the *Bad* album. This was the space where Michael wrote 'I Just Can't Stop Loving You' and there I was, sitting in the room, soaking up the vibe. And writing. Writing and writing.

I love my
coffee!

I've never released music in America. I've never even performed there – which is good in a way, because I can look forward to the chance that the day might still come that I do. But as a place to write music it's my inspiration. Everywhere I look, everything I see, reminds me of the kind of music I aspire to create.

One of the things I love about writing in LA is that sessions never start early! I'm more of a day person than a night owl, unless I'm performing or I'm in the studio, but there's something particularly cool

Recording with co-writer Rich King in LA for the *Angels and Demons* album.

about starting your day slowly with a stroll down Sunset Boulevard. I'll sit outside Starbucks with my first coffee of the day – the weather's always beautiful, of course – and it's then that the buzz starts to build. You can't resist it, watching the beautiful people of LA gliding past, seeing the great cars, hearing the music. Give me a few minutes of that atmosphere and I'm ready to go.

'You can't resist it, watching the beautiful people of LA gliding past, seeing the great cars, hearing the music. Give me a few minutes of that atmosphere and I'm ready to go.'

Chances are, though, that I won't be due in the studio till the afternoon. So I'll head to the gym, do a workout and that'll make me feel even better. LA lends itself to that kind of lifestyle even more than London. People there are fitness fanatics, just like they are in Australia where I grew up, and much more so than in the UK – although, these days, the UK is becoming increasingly health and fitness conscious. So that's another reason for me to feel like I fit in there.

So, I've had my coffee, I've been to the gym. Any minute now I'm going to be called into the studio for my writing session. I might even go down a little early because I want to be there, in the thick of things, because I know I'm going to be surrounded by people who are immersed in what's happening and what's current, right now. So when I get to the studio, it's on, from the beginning. Ideas are flowing. Constantly. I find it easy to tap into my personal experiences, and to express myself through

Left: In LA with my brother Chris and AC Burrell from So Solid Crew, putting the finishing touches to the *Revelation* album.

Opposite: I've always loved being involved in the writing and production of my own recordings.

the music that's flooding out of everywhere.

If I'm lucky, I've got my brothers with me. As you'll find out later in this book, I love having my family around me. They help me get into the vibe. I'll certainly be working with other writers and producers. My own band won't be there, but that doesn't mean I'm not surrounded by musicians. I remember being in one studio in LA when Chris Brown was in the next room recording vocals. All his musicians were there and, before you know it, we're all hanging out together, chatting, listening to music. Such a great experience, and it's impossible not to feel inspired when you're surrounded by those guys.

So that was exactly the kind of environment that led me to writing, and recording, my album *Revelation*. It happened at the Boom Boom Room – a super-cool studio in Burbank, California, owned by Will Smith – over a period of six months in 2008. It was an emotional period in my life, for reasons that have been well-documented elsewhere, but the process of recording that album was a totally inspiring and positive one. It turned out to be one of my favourite records, and an important one for me, because it went close to double platinum in the UK,

and hit number three in the album charts. The songs on that record are very personal to me, and it was thanks to the incredible creative vibe of LA that I managed to channel those feelings into my songwriting.

Recording *Revelation* in Los Angeles was an awesome experience, but for a performer, it's all about bringing it to a live audience. I couldn't wait to take these songs on the road back in the UK.

The tour that followed the release of *Revelation* was set for the second half of 2010, and it was a big one. Probably my biggest up until that point. An arena tour with a few theatre dates thrown in for good measure. I'd had a year and a half of being single, I had a bunch of great songs and I was preparing to take an awesome show on the road. Life should have been rosy. And up to a point it was, except for one nagging problem.

I was tired.

I'm not talking occasionally sleepy. I'm talking moments of sudden, physical exhaustion at times when, ordinarily, I would have been fizzing with energy. I was uncomfortable. My body was aching. In rehearsals for the show I found myself unable to focus properly. I'd get halfway through a song and I'd have to sit down to rest. If you were to meet me, you'd know how out of character that is. Normally I'm bouncing with enthusiasm. For me not to be able to get through a song – well, that means something's just not right.

The guys in the band noticed something was wrong. They kept asking me if I was OK. And the truth was: I wasn't.

My first thought was a deeply worrying one. A little voice in my head started saying that maybe it was my age. I was approaching forty. Maybe I was just getting too old. Maybe things were catching up with me. Maybe I was no longer suited to life on the road!

But that surely couldn't be right? I was fit. I was in good shape. I hadn't been working out all my life for nothing. More to the point, it had only been a couple of years since I'd run a marathon and I was pretty sure my fitness was still at a similar level to how it had been then.

And there was something else: a nagging pain in the side of my stomach. Maybe that was something to do with it? I figured I'd better get it checked out.

If you're worried about your health, and you want to get the best treatment available, you go and get yourself checked out, right? Well, that's what I thought, and that's what I did. I went to see a GP on Harley Street. He gave me the once-over and told me – although not in so

Top: The *Revelation* album launch for media and industry personnel. The album reached number three in the UK chart and almost went double platinum.

Bottom: With my trusted friend and manager for twenty years. Claire is like a sister to me.

many words – that I was being a bit of a hypochondriac. There was absolutely nothing wrong with me. I was probably just a bit tired. All I needed to do was get some rest and take some vitamins.

Was that really all it was? I had my doubts, and I've never been much of a one for vitamin pills – I take the view that if you eat good food and plenty of it, you're going to get all the good stuff you need. But, in fairness, I probably was more of a hypochondriac then than I am now. And who am I to ignore the diagnosis of a Harley Street doctor, or any doctor for that matter? So I went away, I took my vitamins and I carried on with rehearsals for the tour just the same as before, telling myself that the pain would soon go, and my vitality would return.

It didn't. Far from it. The pain grew worse. Much worse. You don't need the gory details, but it became uncomfortable to go to the gents and my general sense of fatigue was off the scale.

I went to another GP. He did an X-ray, examined it carefully and again sent me away with a clean bill of health. If anything, he said, I was overtired and needed to rest. I couldn't rest, of course. I had a gruelling arena tour to prepare for, so I threw myself straight back into my work. Maybe that would take my mind off things.

The first date of the tour was fast approaching. The closer we got to the opening night, the worse I felt. Going to the bathroom was now extremely uncomfortable. Although I was exhausted, I couldn't sleep properly. I became incredibly agitated, and probably not great to be around. Going to rehearsals became nothing but a chore. Just getting through the day was hell …

And then, before I knew it, it was the eve of the first show. We were in the West Country. The tour was going to kick off in Plymouth the following night, and we were put up in a nearby hotel. The tour was sold out. In twenty-four hours I was going to step out on to the stage and do what I love best. It should have been a fun, buzzing, exciting time. But it wasn't. I could barely concentrate on anything. I was in absolute agony. To make things worse, I'd noticed a little lump in the side of my stomach. Surely that wasn't right? I was beginning to panic.

> 'In twenty-four hours I was going to step out on to the stage and do what I love best. It should have been a fun, buzzing, exciting time. But it wasn't. I could barely concentrate on anything. I was in absolute agony.'

I went to my brother Chris and my road manager, Carl. Carl has been with me for five years and has become a good and trusted friend. I told them what was wrong.

Chris and Carl listened carefully. Then, they said the only thing they could have said: 'Mate, we've been to the doctor twice. They've given you the all-clear.'

'But something just doesn't feel right,' I said.

'Well, bro, you get yourself a good night's sleep and everything will be OK.'

I took their advice, went back to my room and got my head down. I even managed to get a little sleep. But at one in the morning, I woke up.

The pain in my stomach was off the scale. The whole world was a blur. I knew something was terribly wrong. In blinding agony, I crawled across my bed and fumbled for my phone. Somehow I managed to dial Carl's number. I don't remember what I said. In truth, I think I was barely able to speak – Carl was only able to understand fragments of what I was

The pain in my stomach was off the scale. The whole world was a blur. I knew something was terribly wrong.'

saying. I was passing in and out of consciousness as I tried to talk to him.

Chris and Carl burst into my room. They arrived just in time to see me collapse.

The next thing I knew, I was in a hospital room. I didn't know where it was. I didn't know what time it was. All I knew was that I was in a massive amount of pain. The room drifted in and out of focus. I was half-aware of a nurse with a worried face looking down at me. 'You've got a lot of blood in your urine,' she told me. 'We can't treat you here. We need to get you to a bigger hospital. Now.'

I blacked out again.

I've no memory of being moved. No memory of any of the events that followed. All I know is that it was an extremely dangerous situation. Potentially career-shortening. Even life-threatening. But in a perverse kind of way, it was the best thing that ever happened to me.

I woke up the next day. I was in a new hospital bed, at Musgrove Park Hospital in Taunton. And for the first time in months, the pain that had been my constant companion was no longer there. And sitting by my bedside was the person who may well have saved my life. His name was Dr Ruaraidh MacDonagh (pronounced 'Rory'). I had no way of knowing, as I met him for that first time lying in my hospital bed, just how important he and his family would become in my life.

'Well,' he said. 'It was a bit tough, but we got rid of it.'

I blinked. 'Got rid of *what*?' I asked.

Dr MacDonagh explained that I'd had a kidney stone. But not an ordinary kidney stone. This one was a ureteric stone, lodged in the tube between the kidney and the bladder. The kidney was blocked and becoming septic. If it had gone on for any longer, the results could have been disastrous. If left untreated, the kidney on that side might have failed altogether. And if the sepsis had not been treated, it could have been life-threatening. But thanks to Dr MacDonagh, everything was going to be OK. 'You're going to feel a bit strange for a while,' he told me, 'but you'll be fine.'

'If it had gone on for any longer, the results could have been disastrous. If left untreated, the kidney on that side might have failed altogether. And if the sepsis had not been treated, it could have been life-threatening.'

It was music to my ears, but it didn't make sense. I'd been to two GPs. I'd had an X-ray. I'd been given the all-clear, twice! Dr MacDonagh could hardly believe it. 'It's quite easy to see on the scan,' he told me. 'Unfortunately the X-ray you had previously was not the correct one to show kidney stones.'

I was so relieved. Pain-free for the first time in months, all I could think of was jumping out of bed and getting to the show that evening. It would be tight, but I could make it. Then Dr MacDonagh dropped a bombshell. 'At the least, you need to rest for two weeks – ideally, you should rest for six weeks.'

I stared at him. 'I can't,' I said. 'I've got a show tonight.' And you know what they say: the show must go on.

Dr MacDonagh smiled. 'There's no way,' he said, 'that you're going on stage tonight, or any night for the next two weeks. You've just had a major operation and you need to rest.'

'But the tour's sold out,' I pleaded.

Dr MacDonagh shrugged. 'You'll have to cancel it.'

Now, to cancel a major, nationwide arena tour is far more easily said than done. Even cancelling a single night is pretty much out of the question. It's a logistical nightmare, because you have to find everyone who's paid for a ticket and give them their money back. It's also a bad idea because it means that next time you do a tour, people are less likely to commit to coming along, because they think you're unreliable. But these weren't the real reasons I didn't want to cancel anything. The truth is that, when people have bought tickets to your show, the chances are that they've spent a lot of money and they've been waiting excitedly for a long time. I'm nobody special. I'm certainly not at the level of some of the greats of showbusiness. I'm well aware that Peter Andre cancelling a show is not like Frank Sinatra cancelling a show. But still, I have my fans and I have a following. To cancel a show – let alone a tour – would mean disappointing many tens of thousands of people.

In the end, I was persuaded to reschedule the first show. I would return to Plymouth at the end of the tour. But I was adamant that the rest of the tour would go ahead. 'I can't bail out,' I told the doctor. 'I just can't.'

'You're a tough cookie, aren't you?' He smiled at me.

Tough, or reckless, I'm not sure which. Whatever the truth, as I lay there talking to Dr MacDonagh, I felt an overwhelming sense of gratitude towards this man who had brought me back from the brink. In fact, it went deeper than that. This guy was like Jesus to me! I was so grateful, I found I couldn't stop thanking him. 'Please, tell me how I can repay you.'

He waved me away. 'Don't worry about it, you're fine.'

'But I want to repay you in some way. Can I get you tickets for the show?'

On the *Revelation*
tour, still recovering
from my operation.

The *Revelation* tour was a big-budget arena tour, which saw everything from elaborate dance routines to pyrotechnics to hydraulic staging. No wonder I found it difficult to obey doctor's orders and stay still.

And probably more to keep me quiet than for any other reason, he said, 'Yeah, that would be great. I'll bring the family along.'

So it was that the MacDonagh family was scheduled to come to the postponed Plymouth show later in the year. In the meantime, I had a tour to think about.

I suppose it's only natural that the next few days are a bit of a blur. I'd just undergone major surgery and, like the good doctor said, I really should have been resting. But I do have a very clear memory of being on stage the following day. Everyone in the audience knew I'd just had an operation, and I'm sure that if they knew exactly what state I was in, they'd have been very understanding if I'd postponed that night too. I was all patched up, an enormous dressing along the right-hand side of my abdomen, and the wound had a nasty habit of oozing blood when I moved. Put it this way: it's a good job my stage outfit was black!

Dr MacDonagh had read me the riot act. If I was to go on stage, I was to stay as still as possible. I wasn't to move around too much. Well, anyone who's seen me perform will know that's not my style, but I did my best to follow his instructions. I knew that show inside out. I carried it. I knew where every stab from the horns was going to come in, where every lighting hit was. Ordinarily, I'd have been all over the stage, in perfect sync with my musicians. As it was, I could do little more than stand there pointing and making the occasional hand gesture in time with the band. It gave the show a bit of movement, a bit of rhythm, but it was nothing like it was supposed to be.

Following doctor's orders didn't last long. I soon started to get itchy feet. Night by night, I moved a little bit more, each movement a little bit bigger. Within two weeks I was doing full-on dance routines. It was silly, really. I was careful, but nowhere near as careful as I should have been. Anything could have happened – the wound could have split or

'Following doctor's orders didn't last long. I soon started to get itchy feet. Night by night, I moved a little bit more, each movement a little bit bigger. Within two weeks I was doing full-on dance routines.'

become infected. I could have put myself in a position where I'd have to cancel a whole load more shows. But what can I say? Sometimes, when you have that drive to perform and there's an audience out there watching you, it's almost impossible not to throw yourself into the performance ...

I kept in touch with Dr MacDonagh – or Ru, as I now called him. I was probably a little over the top. I just couldn't stop thanking him for everything he'd done for me. I know it sounds crazy but, in my eyes, there really was something a little bit saint-like about him. He'd brought me back from the dead! And so I was looking forward to catching up with him again when the time came for me to perform the postponed show in Plymouth. By now, the rest of the tour was done and dusted, the wound from my operation was healing nicely and I felt like I was in pretty good shape. Ru called me the night before the show. 'I'm sending my wife and daughter down,' he told me. 'Would it be OK if they came to the soundcheck?'

Well, of course it was OK. This guy had given me my life back. The very least I could do was meet his family. I was looking forward to it.

And so it was that, the following day, Emily MacDonagh walked into my soundcheck, and into my life.

Emily

'I looked across the table at Emily and I was suddenly struck by how absolutely stunning she was.'

Emily

If you ask her now, Emily will tell you that she wasn't expecting much from that show in Plymouth. Like a lot of people do, she thought she was in for an evening of cheesy pop. But, as most people also do, she later told me that she was blown away. It's something I've grown used to. Before my shows, I do 'meet and greets', where I have the opportunity to say hi to some of my fans. Often, there will be a sheepish-looking guy and I'll say to him, 'You were dragged here by your missus, right?' When these guys admit that's true, as they usually do, I make them a promise: 'Mate, by the end of tonight, you're going to love it.'

Because here's the thing. There are a lot of different sides to my career. There's the singing. There's the dancing. There's the TV presenting and reality shows. I'm really not one to blow my own trumpet. You'll never hear me bigging myself up about any of those things. I know there are better singers out there, and better dancers. But where I will praise myself – where I think I shine, and where I feel I can stand alongside pretty much anyone – is as a performer.

I hear a lot of people saying: how can Peter Andre be so successful on the back of just one song? It doesn't matter that I've had three number-one songs, a number-one album and multi-platinum records in the UK and abroad. The truth is that people only really remember 'Mysterious Girl' (which is not a bad thing as the song was a massive success). So the

'I know there are better singers out there, and better dancers. But where I will praise myself – where I think I shine, and where I feel I can stand alongside pretty much anyone – is as a performer.'

fact that I'm still lucky enough to be selling out big arena tours must be down to something else. And that something else, I would like to think, is the performance. The showmanship. I come from the old school – the generation of performers who believe that if you're going to go out on stage, you need to be the full package. You have to know how to sing, dance, act, interact with the audience – the works. And that's why I can pretty much guarantee that anyone who comes down to one of my gigs is going to have a great night. Those guys dragged along to the shows by their wives and girlfriends? Their reaction is almost always the same: 'That was totally not what I expected. It blew me away.' And it's that reaction that keeps my shows selling, so thank you, everyone.

I completely understand why people think that way, because I do it myself. A couple of years back, I was invited by Peter Fincham, who was then the head of ITV, to sing at a charity gig. I got up on stage, did my thing, and Peter said, 'You know, I've never got it before, but now I get it.' However, I was sharing the bill with another well-known singer and I found myself doing to him exactly what people do to me. 'Yeah, I know he can sing, but can I really be bothered to listen to him?' But I did, and he was really great.

Emily MacDonagh didn't have the highest hopes for the show. She came along because there was a free ticket, thinking that it might be a bit of a laugh, but I don't think she expected to enjoy it as much as she did. We met backstage, along with her mum. At that time I can honestly say that neither of us had romance on our minds. But I remember, quite clearly, thinking: what an amazingly good-looking family! There was clearly more to them than good looks, however. They were also incredibly – there's no other word for it – *nice*. They were polite. Friendly. Just great people to be around. I made the decision right there that these were people I wanted to have in my life. I wanted both of our families to be friends.

'I made the decision right there that these were people I wanted to have in my life. I wanted both of our families to be friends.'

Over the weeks and months that followed, we kept in touch. I couldn't stop myself from calling Ru now and again to thank him for everything he'd done. He was typically modest. 'Would you stop,' he'd say to me. 'It's what I do!' But with good humour he put up with my constant desire to show my gratitude, and the rest of the family put up with my occasional phone calls. When it transpired, some months later, that I would be in the West Country, Ru invited me over for dinner at their home in Taunton.

I remember that evening vividly. I sat at the table, surrounded by Emily, her four brothers and her mum and dad. It was like something out of a movie. They were the archetypal polite English family. There were no phones in sight and there was complete harmony as they sat around, chatting and eating. Emily's mum, Rebecca – also a doctor – had cooked an incredible meal, and this quintessentially English family were all clearly extremely intelligent. Emily was training to be a doctor too and everyone

My rock, my friend, my
beautiful wife, Emily.
We're two peas in a pod.

else around the table was either a doctor also or a mathematician! Truth to tell, I felt rather out of place, coming as I did from the entertainment industry, which was so far removed from their lives.

As I sat with this amazing family, I looked across the table at Emily and I was suddenly struck by how absolutely stunning she was. There was something about her that made me feel like a teenager again. She was so beautiful – she reminded me of Brooke Shields (I know, I know, some of you younger ones are thinking, 'Who's Brooke Shields ...?'). It seemed silly to imagine that she'd be interested in someone like me. I put that thought from my mind, but I did give her my number. 'If you ever wanted to call me, just to say hello,' I suggested. 'And if you're ever in the area, come over and meet the family.'

Despite the initial attraction, it was honestly never meant to be anything other than a friendship. We began communicating regularly – not just Emily and me, but the whole MacDonagh family. And when Emily *was* in the neighbourhood, she *did* drop by to say hello – sometimes with a friend, sometimes with her brothers, sometimes on her own. They met my kids and instantly took a shine to them. The feeling was mutual – my kids grew to love Emily and her family, whom I'd take them to visit whenever I had a show down that way. We were all becoming firm friends.

Over the next year and a half, Emily and I became best buddies, hanging out in the way that best friends do. On one occasion I was painting the house, and she offered to come and give me a hand. On other occasions, she'd be heading up to London with friends and would stop over at my place on the way. It was never anything romantic. We weren't a couple. I'd be lying if I said I didn't occasionally look at her and think, yet again: she *is* pretty stunning. But in the same thought I'd tell myself: forget it. I certainly had too much respect for her to toy with her affections. And who was I to think that she might be remotely interested in me anyway?

An amazing thing was happening over that time, though. A love story was blossoming, slowly and organically. By the time I had started thinking to myself that I really could be with this woman for the rest of my life, we had built something solid and lasting: a true friendship.

'An amazing thing was happening over that time, though. A love story was blossoming, slowly and organically.'

In the same way that Emily's family is quintessentially British, my mum and dad are very traditionally Greek Cypriot. They are also devout Jehovah's Witnesses.

I have nothing but admiration for my parents' faith, and nothing but love for some of the wonderful things they taught us as a result of it. I know people have their own opinion on religion, but my mum and dad live their life by the Bible and as a result they always taught us to love everybody and to be respectful of everybody. They also taught us, however, that when it comes to being a Witness, you either sit at the table of God, or you sit at the table of the world. You can't do both. They never forced us to make that decision. We were not baptized as children. Instead, they waited for us to become old enough to make the choice for ourselves, the reason being that, once you're baptized, and you've given your life to God, you have to abide by the rules. By the time I was a teenager, partying behind my parents' back – sorry, Mum and Dad! – I knew that I was going to be living too worldly a life to do that. And certainly, by the time I was doing music and had started making slightly racy videos, I knew there was no way that I could follow the Witness lifestyle, even though I had nothing but respect for the faith.

I was honoured to be made the cultural ambassador to Valletta, Malta. Emily and I had the great pleasure of meeting some of the dignitaries when we visited in 2013.

Of course, that has never stopped my mum from wanting the same thing for me as she did when I was a boy. In the world view of a traditional Greek-Cypriot mother, a Greek boy is supposed to marry a Greek girl. Growing up, all I ever heard from my mum was, 'Peter, you've got to marry a Greek girl!' And if the Greek girl happened to be a Witness, so much the better. Of course, growing up in a remote part of Australia, Greek Witness girls were pretty thin on the ground. In any case, even though this was my mum's dream for me, and I respected her for that, it really was never on the cards for me to marry a Greek Jehovah's Witness.

'In the world view of a traditional Greek-Cypriot mother, a Greek boy is supposed to marry a Greek girl. Growing up, all I ever heard from my mum was, "Peter, you've got to marry a Greek girl!"'

So when I told my mum that I was getting very friendly with the wonderful MacDonagh family, and especially with Emily, and said I'd like her to meet them, she was kind of reluctant. I suppose she just didn't want to be put in an awkward situation, but I was persistent and eventually she agreed to come and have a coffee with Emily.

I've never known such a reaction from my mum. She took me to one side. *'Ine goukla ...'* she said in Greek. 'This girl is *beautiful!*' I don't remember my mum *ever* saying something like that, unless she was talking about a Greek girl from some village in Cyprus, probably the daughter of a goatherd, that she wanted me to marry!

I had a similar experience with my dad. I had told him how this Jesus-like surgeon had saved me. How he was like my guardian angel. (I told you I was a bit over the top!) Dad said he'd like to meet him, and soon enough he had the opportunity, because he developed a medical problem and Emily's dad performed a very complicated operation on him. So now, my father had the same opinion of Ru as I did. And when the time came for him to meet the rest of the MacDonaghs, he took me to one side. 'Peter, they are a good family. I would be happy for you to be with this family!'

I can't emphasize enough how unusual this was. As a teenager, I'd either felt obliged to keep my girlfriends secret, or I'd find myself thrusting them upon my mum and dad. I'd certainly always already be in a relationship before introducing anyone to my parents. But now things had been turned upside down. I wasn't in a relationship with Emily. We were just really great friends. But my mum and dad loved her, and here they were telling me: she's the one! And she wasn't even Greek, or a Witness, or even a goatherd's daughter (although she did grow up in the countryside!).

By now, I was beginning to think along the same lines as my mum and dad. I realized I had genuine feelings for Emily. But because the MacDonaghs were such a proper family, and because I had such respect for her and her parents, I felt honour-bound to go about everything the right way. And so, before I even brought up the subject with Emily, I decided I had to do the traditional thing and call her dad. I wanted to ask his permission to take things to the next level, and to assure him that my intentions towards his daughter were strictly honourable and respectful.

The MacDonaghs and I were staying at The May Fair hotel in London for a charity event when I made the call.

We always love to
attend the Pride of
Britain Awards.
There are so many
unsung heroes.

I don't mind admitting I was pretty nervous. And even more nervous when he answered. I asked the question rather sheepishly. 'Ru ... is it OK with you if I ask Emily to be my partner?'

There was a silence. Then, straight as a die, he said: 'What, do you mean like a dance partner?'

'No,' I replied hesitantly. 'Not a dance partner. I mean ...'

I heard him laugh at the other end of the phone and realized that he was just joking around. Relief crashed over me. 'Course you can, you 'nana,' he said. 'I always knew it was on the cards for you guys. You should give it a go. Date for six months, see how you feel after that.'

Now it was my turn to be silent. 'No, Ru,' I said after a moment, 'I don't think you understand. I'm serious. I've got too much respect for her just to try and "go out" with her. I've known her for two years already, we're best friends and I'm not mucking about.' I wasn't overstating things. I knew that if Emily and I got together, there was every chance that it would lead to marriage.

So, having gained Ru's permission to ask his daughter out, I did just that. Emily said yes, and it felt like everything was clicking into place. That night we announced to our family and friends that we were a couple. It was all very official. Very old school. But I think we both liked it that way.

I never liked referring to Emily as my 'girlfriend'. It sounded so temporary, when I knew I was in this for the long haul. It didn't take me long to realize that she was perfect for me. I wanted to be sure that she felt the same. I sat her down one day early in our relationship and said, 'Look, I'm probably a bit different to some of your friends. For some people, their idea of a good time is to go out partying all night, stagger home the next day, or spend the whole weekend drinking. But I've got to be honest: I got all my partying out of my system in my twenties. That way of life just isn't me.'

My fortieth birthday
celebrations – with a
cake fit for Liberace.

'Thank God for that,' Emily told me with a smile. 'Me neither.'

It was further evidence that we were two peas in a pod, and that the things that were important to me were important to her, too. However, anyone who is a parent will know what I mean when I say that, once your children come along, they become *the* most important thing in your life. So it was with my son and daughter, Junior and Princess. As a single dad, it was crucial to me that, when they were with me, as they are half the time, they didn't see me coming home with a string of different girlfriends. I kept that part of my life separate, until Emily came along. I wanted them to understand the meaning of commitment, and for their home life to be as stable and ordinary as possible, given that their dad's job meant he was often in the public eye. Up until the time Emily and I got together, they had only ever seen me kiss one woman, and that was their mother.

Although I pretty much knew from the moment we were together that Emily was 'the one', it didn't mean I was about to break that rule. Whenever the kids were with us, we slept in different rooms. We never kissed in front of them. We never even held hands. Behaving like this was so important to me. I didn't really think for a moment that things wouldn't work out between me and Emily – we had committed to each other as a couple, and things were going great – but if they didn't, my first thought was that the kids shouldn't be confused.

So, as our relationship blossomed, the kids only knew her as a friend. But what a friend. Just as Emily and I had developed this incredible closeness, so the children were creating an amazing bond with her. When the time came and I knew I was going to ask Emily to marry me, my kids had truly grown to love her, so I had no worries about sitting down with them and explaining 'the situation'.

Opposite: These two bring such joy to my life, and keep me so young.

'As our relationship blossomed, the kids only knew her as a friend. But what a friend. Just as Emily and I had developed this incredible closeness, so the children were creating an amazing bond with her.'

I'll never forget that chat. 'I want you to know,' I told them, 'that you'll only ever have one mum and one dad. But I really love Emily, and we're together.'

My son rolled his eyes. 'Er, yeah? And?'

I was a bit taken aback. 'What do you mean, "Yeah, and?"'

'Do you think we're stupid?' he asked.

'Of course I don't think you're stupid. But you're only eight years old!'

'So? I already knew you guys were together.'

'How did you know that?' I thought we'd been pretty subtle about it all.

'It's obvious,' he said. 'You guys can't stop looking at each other!'

Out of the mouths of babes ...

Any worries I had that the kids might have a problem with Emily and me being a couple went out of the window that day. In fact, they were positively enthusiastic, and started egging me on to propose to her. They became obsessed with me marrying her, because they loved her too. I would refer to her as Auntie Ems, and they'd shout at me, 'She's not our auntie, Dad! She's our stepmum!' And this was before we even got married ...

Some people told Emily she was crazy getting involved with a single guy who had a young family, and all the baggage that came with it. But I think she knew from the beginning that it wasn't like that. She loved the kids, and wanted to become a friend figure to them. Just as she and I had established this mutual understanding and companionship in the eighteen months before we became a couple, so Emily and the kids had become the best of friends before their relationship moved on to something deeper.

Everything was good. We had what so many new families in our situation don't have: a bedrock of friendship that would, we hoped, see us through the good times and the bad.

It turned out that we were going to need it.

A lot of people say that Junior looks so much like me, but pictures of me at Bista's age – wow!

Brotherly Love

'They were, and are, our rock. We love
them completely. My brothers and sister and
I would have had no joy in our lives if it
wasn't for our parents.'

Brotherly Love

By now, you've probably got the idea that family is very important to me. I come from a large family, and we've been through a lot. I was the baby. I've one sister – Debbie – and four brothers – Michael, Danny, Chris and Andrew. Not all siblings are as close as we are – my brothers and sister are my best friends – and when we were young we had good reason to stick together.

I was born and spent my earliest years in Harrow, north-west London. It was a good place for a Greek-Cypriot family to be, because it was a very multicultural area. Pakistani families rubbed shoulders with Jewish families, Italians with Jamaicans, Spanish with Greeks. We were all the same, because we were all different.

One day, it all changed. There was a street fight just outside our house. I was too young to remember it very well, but I'm told it was a bloodbath. After that, everything was different. The area became much rougher than it had been before. Mum and Dad, whose first priority was always their family, felt that it wasn't a safe place for us to be any more. They started to think that we should move on.

It was around this time – I was six years old – that Mum and Dad went on a three-month holiday to Australia. They took Debbie with them, but we boys went to live with our paternal grandmother. Now, Greek parents such as ours can be very strict. Jehovah's Witness Greek parents, even stricter. My mum and dad had these two binding sets of rules that they, and we, had to adhere to: the traditional Greek rules, and the Witness rules. When I look back on my childhood, not for a single moment do I hold a grudge against them for that strictness. They were, and are, our rock. We love them completely. My brothers and sister and I would have had no joy in our lives if it wasn't for our parents. Even now, and even though they live many thousands of miles away in Australia, they're the cornerstone of our lives. Not a day passes when one of us doesn't speak with them. They are everything to us.

For this reason, I clearly remember experiencing a mixture of emotions when they went away. We were excited, of course. My grandmother was a fun, easygoing lady. There wouldn't be the same strictness in the household while we were living with her in charge. I suppose I probably also felt a little bit jealous that Mum, Dad and Debbie were going on what seemed to be a very exciting adventure. I was also

At six months old I was already a style icon!

sad. As my parents were so strict, I think I had already learned a lesson, the truth of which would become very clear to me when I had kids of my own. It is this: children need boundaries. They *like* boundaries. Because when you have boundaries, you feel protected. When those boundaries are taken away, it can be kind of scary.

'As my parents were so strict, I think I had already learned a lesson, the truth of which would become very clear to me when I had kids of my own. It is this: children need boundaries.'

Three months is a long time when you're six years old. Although it was fun, in a way, not having my parents around and being given what was, I suppose, my first real taste of relative freedom, that time was a bit of a blur. Deep down, I'm sure I couldn't wait for them to get back. I needed that strictness in my life. And I'm certain that those three months brought me and my brothers much closer together as a family unit.

When my parents returned from Sydney, it was with momentous news for the Andréa family. Mum and Dad had decided that we were to emigrate to Australia. They had come to the decision that there was a better life to be had for us in Sydney than on the streets of north-west London. Once again, I remember my mind being a riot of mixed emotions. On the one hand, we were off to live in the sunshine, by the sea. With the exception of a few family holidays to Cyprus, this was something we'd hardly ever experienced before. I can still recall the excitement I felt at that prospect. On the other hand, it meant leaving my Sri Lankan girlfriend

At Botany Bay in Australia, where Captain Cook landed. This picture was taken when I was six years old, with my sister, Debbie, and my brother Danny in the background.

Miranda — she was also six — along with all my other friends. I was going to miss them. Even more, I was going to miss my brother Andrew. He was twenty-two at the time. He'd got married and had moved on in life. But he was still my big brother, and I was saddened by the prospect of being parted by a distance of ten thousand miles.

The moment we landed in Sydney is etched in my memory. I remember being blasted by the heat, and thinking that I was just about to embark upon the biggest holiday of my life. I guess it was difficult for a six-year-old to grasp the magnitude of what we were doing. The idea was always that we should live in Sydney, where my dad had family. Soon after we moved there, however, one of my parents' friends said to him, 'I want you to come and see this place called the Gold Coast.'

Distances are big in Australia. The Gold Coast from Sydney is about an hour by plane, but it's about ten hours by car. Nevertheless, Mum and Dad drove all the way there. They were amazed by what they found. The Gold Coast was a paradise. In fact, they call it 'Surfer's Paradise'. There were clear, blue skies and beautiful golden beaches stretching off into the distance. When they saw this place, my parents' reaction was instant: 'This is it, we're going to move here.'

And so, as a family, we moved to paradise. It turned out, however, that paradise had its dark side.

We found a house to move into. Back in London, Mum had been a seamstress and Dad a barber. They had also owned several properties – houses in Barons Court and Notting Hill, as well as a barber shop and a clothes shop in Paddington – so they were quite business-minded. When we arrived on the Gold Coast, Mum and Dad bought a couple of clothes shops – they were quite cheap to buy at the time – and that was it: we were residents. And of course, beautiful though the Gold Coast was, this was not quite the holiday I expected it to be. There was no getting away

Possibly one of my worst hairstyles to date, from when I was at school on the Gold Coast in Australia.

from the fact that I had to go to school. And school was where it started to go wrong.

The song 'Wherever I Lay My Hat (That's My Home)' – recorded by Paul Young – was popular at the time. I was recently lucky enough to meet Paul, and had the opportunity to tell him that to this day I find that a particularly poignant song. It came to symbolize what turned into a bit of a lonely time for me. School was a different world to what I'd been used to. I'd come from a multicultural city. I was used to different types of people – Indians, black people, white people, Asians – living together quite happily. On the Gold Coast, however, foreigners were a rarity. It was all blond-haired, blue-eyed, good-looking Australians. I had curly black hair, a big nose and an English accent. Worst of all, I was Greek. It made me a complete outcast.

I'd never heard the word 'wog' before. In Australia, it's a derogatory term for Greeks and Italians. I heard that word a lot on the Gold Coast.

It wasn't just the kids who racially abused me. The teachers did it too. I remember sitting in a lesson and one of the teachers saying, 'You're not going to get far in my class, you greasy wog. Greasy wogs aren't welcome here ...'

The kids were more violent in their abuse. On one occasion they tied me to a fence, then took it in turns to throw stones at my head. I don't need to tell you how much that hurt, or how scared I was. For a while, I tried to put up with it. But there's only so much a young kid can cope with. I told Mum and Dad what was going on. They were massively concerned, of course, but they told me not to worry, and that things would settle down.

They didn't. Not for me, nor for my brothers. In fact, things got progressively worse. Even if I did manage to make the occasional friend, they'd turn on me in an instant if the guys in the playground decided to pick on me, which they often did. Even out of school, the racism was relentless. You'd walk down the street and people would call you everything under the sun. And being a Jehovah's Witness family didn't help things. We were, in every respect, outsiders.

Looking back, I try to understand why people thought of us and behaved towards us the way they did. I think it was because we were literally like aliens to them. There were no ethnic minorities on the Gold Coast at that time – it was nothing like England – and my family and I truly were the only weird-looking 'greasy wogs' around (I'm sure my bros would say, 'Speak for yourself!').

So we stuck together. When I was having trouble, my brothers would muscle in and fight on my behalf. I didn't really want them to do that at the time. It just escalated the situation. The bullies would get *their* brothers involved, and before you knew it the whole thing had turned more horrible than it had been before. At the same time, however, I think I must, in some way, have felt like they were saving my life. I really was getting beaten black and blue in that school playground. We even found ourselves having to call ourselves by a different name. The kids in the playground would call us *Andrea* – like the girl's name – rather than Andréa. It was Mike's idea that we start calling ourselves plain 'Andre'.

When you bond with people in times of adversity, those bonds can become unusually strong. For example, after a couple years the unimaginable happened and another Greek boy appeared in the playground. Like me, he had dark hair and a big nose and we became best friends instantly. His name was George Nicolaou, and he experienced exactly the same persecution as I did. We were both outsiders. We were

Seventeen years old and dreaming of a life on the stage.

My brother Michael and me in LA, on set for the video of 'All About Us', which I recorded with Montell Jordan and released in 1997.

both bullied. We went through very tough times together. As a result, we became so close that, more than thirty years later, he would be the best man at my wedding.

The same process was happening with me and my brothers. The reason we are so very close now is because, way back then, we had each other's backs. No matter what would happen later in our lives, that bond, which became rock-solid in adversity, would remain. They became my very closest friends.

As time passed, things started to improve. I decided that I wanted to learn kung fu. My dad wouldn't allow it. He couldn't understand why, if I wanted to be a peaceful person, I wanted to learn to fight. I tried to explain to him that I was actually learning how to defend myself. He still couldn't understand, and I can see his point of view with the benefit of hindsight. At the time, however, it meant I had to go behind his back. I went to the gym with my brothers, but, as always, they were looking out for me and wouldn't let me do weights because I was so skinny. Instead, I used to do countless sit-ups, then get to work on a punch bag. Gradually I did learn to defend myself and, yes, how to fight. Little by little, the guys who had taken such delight in picking on me began to understand that I wasn't a pushover. They backed off. At the same time, the ethnic minority population of the school started to increase – not just Greek kids, but Italians and Lebanese too – so I wasn't such a curiosity.

As the racism eased off, the bond between us brothers remained unbreakable. It was particularly strong for me because I was the youngest. There was a pecking order in our family: you respected and gave way to your older sibling. If there was a spare seat in the front of the car, for example, the older brother got it. It was just the way things were. Michael, Debbie and I were all of a similar age, and we became very close because of that. When Andrew was away, which he almost always was because

My family has always been my life. My beloved mother and father have recently celebrated their sixtieth wedding anniversary. Words can't describe how much they mean to me.
From left to right: Chris, Junior, Michael, Princess, me, Debbie, Debbie's son Savandy, Mum and Dad.

he had a family of his own in the UK, Chris, the second eldest, was the big brother. Chris was often travelling back and forth from England himself, so when he was away, Danny was like the big brother.

'As the racism eased off, the bond between us brothers remained unbreakable. It was particularly strong for me because I was the youngest.'

I started to miss Andrew massively. I had learned, through everything that had happened to us, to appreciate and respect my brothers, and as time went on I started to feel Andrew's absence very keenly. Those occasions when he was with us in Australia stick out in my mind as especially happy ones. Andrew was an animal lover. He was obsessed with little creatures, and he was so articulate about them, like a young David Attenborough. I always said he should be a public speaker. He was fascinating. The ultimate storyteller. As a boy, I would sit transfixed as he explained how important it was to take care of all creatures, even the ones that we considered pests, because they all had a purpose in nature. Andrew was a Witness at the time, like Mum and Dad. He rose to become a ministerial servant – one step down from an elder – by the time he was thirty. And he was a gentle soul. He would not so much as harm a spider, and he encouraged us to behave in the same way.

Top left: The launch of New York Coffee Club. Unbeknown to us, the chemo was taking its toll on my brother Andrew. **Top right**: The three amigos. With my brothers Michael and Andrew, getting into the Mexican spirit for Bista's Mariachi birthday party. **Centre left and right**: There are only three years between me and Michael (I'm younger, in case you're wondering!). We've always been very close. **Bottom**: My fortieth birthday was just a few months after we lost Andrew. It was a very bittersweet evening. He was, and will always be, missed. From left to right: Danny, me, Chris, Michael.

When I was about twelve, he came to visit us in Australia with his wife and son. He was very keen to chat with his youngest siblings – myself, Debbie and Michael – and one evening's topic of conversation was the importance of frogs. I'd never really been interested in frogs before but somehow, when Andrew started talking about them, you couldn't fail to get swept along with his enthusiasm. He explained all about the dangerous cane toad – how it had been introduced to Australia to eat the cane beetles that were decimating the important sugar cane crops, and how it was very poisonous. If you get too close to a cane toad and spook it, it can squirt a nasty venom into your eyes, which can blind you. Most people would just tell us kids to steer well clear of cane toads, but Andrew infected us with his enthusiasm for even the less lovable of God's creatures. I could have listened to him talk about toads all night.

> 'Andrew was an animal lover. He was obsessed with little creatures, and he was so articulate about them, like a young David Attenborough. I always said he should be a public speaker. He was fascinating. The ultimate storyteller.'

Later that evening, Debbie and I were down by the pool. It must have been nine o'clock, and we suddenly shouted out: 'Andrew! Come quick! There's a cane toad down here!'

Andrew came sprinting out of the house, just as we knew he would.

All aboard! Cruising the Med with my family.

One mention of an interesting creature and he'd be there. 'Where?' he shouted. 'Where is it?'

'Over here!'

We waited until he was right by the pool before we revealed our trick. There was no cane toad, of course. Just two mischievous kids waiting to throw their big brother into the pool, which we did. In the face of our strict upbringing, we had our laughs by being cheeky. Andrew called us a couple of little rascals, but he enjoyed the joke as much as we did. And I think that's part of what made him so special. He was an adult, with a family of his own, but he was still our brother, and eager to do the things that brothers do. And because I was so close to the siblings that I lived with, I felt an urge to be extra-close to the brother whom I wasn't living with. I looked up to him, and could never wait for him to come and visit us. He was always my closest brother. He just happened to be the one who lived furthest away.

This set the tone of my relationship with Andrew for the next thirty years, almost to the point where, even when we were on opposite sides of the world, there seemed to be some kind of connection between us.

Years later, one night in 1996, I was asleep in my apartment in Rotherhithe in London. My brother Chris was staying with me. At two o'clock in the morning I suddenly woke up. I was drenched in cold sweat. I was shaking. Petrified. I clambered out of bed and went to find Chris. 'Bro,' I said, shaking him awake. 'Bro, something's happened.'

Chris stared at me blearily. 'What are you talking about?'

'I'm freaking out,' I told him. 'Something's happened. We've got to call Australia. We've got to call home.'

'Bro, everything's fine. You've just had a bad dream.'

But it was more than that. I knew it was. 'No,' I insisted. 'Something bad's happened.'

'All right,' Chris said. 'Call home.'

So I did.

Minutes before, at about the time I must have woken up, my brother Andrew – who was in Australia with my mum and dad at the time – had been involved in a terrible car crash. He was unbelievably lucky to be alive. Even as I spoke to my dad on the phone, Andrew was being extracted from the wreckage of the crash by the Jaws of Life.

I don't know how to explain what happened that night. No doubt some people would put it down to coincidence. All I can say is this: somehow, despite the ten thousand miles that separated us, I *knew* that my brother was in trouble at that very moment. That's how close we were.

> 'Somehow, despite the ten thousand miles that separated us, I *knew* that my brother was in trouble at that very moment. That's how close we were.'

And that's why, when I eventually lost him, it was the most painful thing that I had ever experienced.

I find it almost unbearably difficult to talk about losing Andrew. I am certainly in two minds about wanting to write about it. I include the pages that follow in the hope that they might help somebody else who finds themselves in the same situation as him. In the hope that something positive can be taken from an event that threatened to rip our family to bits …

Andrew

'*They* are *me*, all of my siblings, equally.
If something were to happen to one of
them, it would be like losing a limb.'

Andrew

It was before Emily and I were even a couple that I first travelled to Zanzibar with her and her family.

Zanzibar is a place of extremes. Some people know it as a stunning paradise with beautiful beaches and perfect scenery. But it's rotten at the core, because the healthcare system is so poor. In recent years there have been three main hospitals in Zanzibar, but they're not hospitals as you or I would imagine them. They have little money, facilities or equipment. Very few doctors. Hundreds of newborn babies die every year in these hospitals, because the staff simply don't have the means to save them.

When Emily's father Ru first heard about and saw the desperate state of the healthcare system in Zanzibar, he felt compelled to do something about it. He founded the charity HIPZ, which stands for Health Improvement Project Zanzibar. The aim of HIPZ is to get the three hospitals in Zanzibar kitted out so that they at least have a fighting chance of providing decent healthcare for the impoverished people of that island. It does this by seeking donations not only of money but also of equipment from the UK. As I write this, HIPZ has already transformed the fortunes of one of these three hospitals. It has saved countless lives. But there is an enormous amount of work still to do.

Once I had become friendly with the MacDonagh family, Ru told me all about the situation in Zanzibar, and about the charity. He persuaded me to go out to Africa with him and witness for myself what was happening there. Maybe I could use my profile to raise some awareness of the charity and its work. Having heard him speak so passionately about it, I decided I definitely wanted to find out some more. So I found myself travelling with Ru, Emily and Emily's mum, Rebecca, along with a camera crew for the reality show I was filming at the time, to Zanzibar to see for myself what was happening there.

Anyone who has ever been to the poorer parts of Africa will know that it really couldn't be further from the comfortable life we live here in the UK. Simply driving along the roads is an eye-opener. We were told that it was very dangerous to drive in Stone Town, the old part of Zanzibar City, because there are no rules of the road. People overtake whenever they want, and cyclists, without any helmets, weave in and out of the traffic on the main road. My attention, however, was not on the dangerous traffic. It was on the kids playing in the rubble by the side of the road. I'd never seen anything like it. They had no shoes to protect themselves from the stony ground. Their trousers were ripped. Their shirts looked like they were sixty years old. It was explained to me that the poor of Zanzibar mostly live in huts made out of clay. They have no electricity and no water. They must walk miles to the nearest tap, fill barrels with water and return with them on their heads. It is as if they are living three thousand years ago. Yet every single one of those kids had a smile on their face as they played in the rubble, or ran along the dirt by the roadside, or kicked about a makeshift ball they'd made out of plastic bags and rubber bands.

During that trip, we visited a school. I've never seen people so content with nothing. Zanzibar is a Muslim society, and these sweet little children wore beautiful white headwear that covered the edges of their faces. They were some of the friendliest, most humble people I've ever

encountered but that school was like no school I'd ever seen. It was in the middle of nowhere. A parched, barren landscape all around. There was no playground or other facilities. Just a squat, square, concrete building, baking under the fierce African sun. When we arrived, the children didn't ask us for money, or food, or drink – although I did have a big bottle of water with me which I shared with them, and which made them think the heavens had opened. The only thing they asked us for was pencils. That told me a lot. All these kids really wanted was an education. They barely even knew what money was, after all.

> 'The only thing they asked us for was pencils. That told me a lot. All these kids really wanted was an education.'

Visiting that school in Zanzibar was a humbling but heartwarming experience. There were lighter moments too. We were staying in a hotel in Stone Town directly opposite Freddie Mercury's family home. We turned up at the hotel and all of a sudden we heard music playing, and the frenzied beating of drums. A party of locals was there to meet us. As I climbed out of the car, with the cameras rolling – we were filming the reality show at the time – our welcoming party put a hat on me and started singing and dancing. They seemed to have it in their heads that Emily and I were a couple, perhaps because we had a film crew with us. It was a strange experience, given that we really were just friends at the

Opposite: Zanzibar has a very special place in my heart. **Top left**: Standing outside Freddie Mercury's house in Stone Town. **Top right**: Visiting one of the hospitals with Dr Emily, Dr Ruaraidh, Dr Rebecca and Dr Chris. **Centre right**: The children of Zanzibar have nothing, and yet are so happy. **Bottom**: Visiting a school to hand out pens and snacks.

time. Emily asked me what was happening. 'Just go with it,' I whispered. I sidled up to Ru and apologized for the mix-up, but he was cool and gave me the same advice I'd just given Emily: 'Go with it!' So it was that we had a little taste of married life before we were even a couple – though once inside the hotel, we were very much in separate rooms. It didn't stop a rumour going round later that we had been secretly married in Africa before our actual wedding, but it was nothing more than that: a rumour.

Such light-hearted moments were more than balanced out by the trip we made to one of the hospitals that HIPZ is trying to improve. As we were driving there, a phone call came through. A woman was about to give birth at the hospital, but there were complications. There were no doctors at the hospital who could help her. The baby's only chance was Ru and Rebecca. They needed to get there as quickly as possible if they were to be of any help.

My memory of that urgent journey is a bit of a blur. We flew along those juddery, dusty roads lined with children playing in the dirt. It took half an hour to get there, but seemed to take three times as long as that. When we arrived, I saw a building that was like no hospital I'd ever seen. It was nothing. Concrete walls and a roof. It was dirty. There were few facilities. No proper maternity ward or outpatients ward. Patients were sitting or lying on the ground outside. It looked like you would imagine a hospital two or three hundred years ago.

Ru and Rebecca tore into this building, their only thought that they had to save this child and its mother. I followed in something of a daze. Before I knew it, I was in the thick of things. Emily was helping her mum and dad – it was the first time I'd seen her at work, and she clearly knew what she was doing. I didn't, but I tried my best, grabbing syringes when I was told to, filling them up with whatever medicine the mother and child needed, while Rebecca administered them. It was frenetic. Chaotic.

With one of the poor mothers who is infected with HIV, and her daughter. Our mission is to improve the hospitals that help people like them.

'Ru and Rebecca tore into this building, their only thought that they had to save this child and its mother. I followed in something of a daze. Before I knew it, I was in the thick of things.'

Everyone was working towards a common aim: to deliver this baby safely, and keep it alive.

We failed. The baby died in Rebecca's arms, in front of my eyes. I'd never seen such a desperately sad thing in my life. As Rebecca gently put one hand over the baby's tiny face, I burst into tears. I couldn't believe that child was gone.

Rebecca and Emily both started to cry, distraught that they hadn't been able to save the baby. I stepped backwards – staggered, more like – and reached out behind me to grab hold of a basin by the wall. My fingers touched something I hadn't expected. It was a blanket. I couldn't understand what it was doing there, so I lifted one corner. Beneath the cloth was another dead baby.

I felt a horrible chill run through my veins. Now that the frenzy had calmed down, I started to look around me a little more carefully. It began to dawn on me that there were dead babies everywhere, covered in blankets. It was almost as if I was standing in the middle of a morgue. It was the most horrific thing I have ever seen.

Ru caught me looking around and said to me, 'Peter, this is why we need to help.' And from that moment on I understood. I'd seen death at close quarters that day, and I would never forget it. Since then, people have asked me why I support Zanzibar when there are charities in the

UK that aim to solve problems much closer to home. All I can say is that if you were to go there, and see what I saw, I'm certain you'd feel compelled to help too. The need to these people is enormous, and it's ongoing. Even as I write this, several years after that first trip to Zanzibar, I have just received a message from Ru to tell me that one of the African orderlies at Kivunge hospital – a woman who was working with HIPZ – has just died very suddenly of AIDS.

> 'If you were to go there, and see what I saw, I'm certain you'd feel compelled to help too. The need to these people is enormous, and it's ongoing.'

Such things happen all the time in Zanzibar. It might look like an island paradise in the holiday brochures, but you only have to scratch the surface to understand that there is a more sinister side to that lovely place. It needs our help.

That would have been one of the most traumatic days of my life, even if nothing else had happened. As we stepped out of the hospital, however, utterly shell-shocked, my phone rang. It was my brother Andrew, calling me all the way from where he was staying with my mum and dad in Australia.

'Hey, bro,' I said, 'how are you?'

There was a short pause. 'Well,' he said. 'Not bad. I've just been to the hospital. I don't want you to worry about it, but they found some cancer cells.'

'What?'

'Don't worry,' he told me. 'It's fine. I just wanted to tell you because, well, I don't really know what it means.'

I collapsed on to the kerb in front of the hospital and burst into tears. There was something in Andrew's voice, something unsaid, that told me this was a lot worse than he was making it sound. I was shocked to the core.

I know a lot of people who aren't that close to their brothers and sisters. But I hope you understand by now that that's not us. When you've got an unbreakable bond because you went through years of bullying and the only people you could rely on were those guys, how can it be? It never mattered to me that Andrew hadn't been around as much when I was a kid. *They* are *me*, all of my siblings, equally. If something were to happen to one of them, it would be like losing a limb. My mum would later explain it better than I ever could. She said: 'If I had to have one of my fingers cut off, which one would hurt less? None of them. They're all the same loss.' And when you're as close a family as we are, it doesn't matter how many brothers or sisters or children you have. Just like the fingers: to lose one of them is the same loss as losing any of them.

I was shocked for another reason. As a family we were under this false, silly illusion that if you don't have cancer in your family, you're not going to get it. I actually believed that if your dad or grandfather hadn't succumbed to the illness, you were safe. We even used to say it to each other: 'Cancer's not in the family.' When we started noticing that certain cousins of ours were being diagnosed with the illness, we rationalized it by telling ourselves that it was probably from a different side of the family. Because cancer was hereditary, wasn't it? Part of the reason I broke down outside that hospital in Zanzibar was because this was the

'When you're as close a family as we are, it doesn't matter how many brothers or sisters or children you have. Just like the fingers: to lose one of them is the same loss as losing any of them.'

first time the word 'cancer' had ever been mentioned with respect to our immediate family.

I could think of only one thing: leaving Zanzibar and getting on the next flight to Australia. I had work commitments, of course, but they could wait. I told my manager, Claire: 'I don't care about work. I'm going home.'

Claire was amazing. She sorted everything out for me while my brother Michael and I got on the first flight that we could. Chris and Danny stayed in the UK – it was more difficult for them to get out of their work commitments – but they were of a similar mindset. 'If anything changes,' they said, 'tell us and we'll get on a plane.'

I'll never forget walking through the front door of my parents' house in Australia. They had kept our arrival a secret from Andrew. My mum, dad and sister hugged us and kissed us – they were so happy to have us there, and by now you probably have an idea of what we big Greek families are like! Andrew was upstairs, so my dad called to him. 'Andrew, there's a letter here for you, you must open it!'

Andrew's voice drifted down the stairs. 'OK, Dad, I'll come down in a minute.'

'No! You must come now! It says "Urgent"!'

Andrew obediently appeared at the top of the stairs. When he saw Michael and me standing there, the emotion on his face was amazing

'I collapsed on to the kerb in front of the hospital and burst into tears. There was something in Andrew's voice, something unsaid, that told me this was a lot worse than he was making it sound. I was shocked to the core.'

to witness. He couldn't believe that we'd travelled all that way to see if he was OK, and we were all so happy to be reunited. It was a great moment.

We did what we could to reassure Andrew that everything was going to be fine. We met with some of his doctors, who explained that he would need to undergo an operation in a couple of weeks to remove the cancer. They seemed fairly sure that they would be able to clear it, as it was only present in one little area, which was cause for optimism. And we did everything we could to enjoy that time as a family. Mum and Dad prepared big barbecues for us, we hung out together and did what we could to act as if everything was normal.

'When he saw Michael and me standing there, the emotion on his face was amazing to witness. He couldn't believe that we'd travelled all that way to see if he was OK, and we were all so happy to be reunited. It was a great moment.'

There was, however, no way of avoiding the shadow that had fallen over us. No way of avoiding the underlying fear that we all felt. Andrew was in a lot of discomfort. He was very tired and often had to take himself away to go to sleep. As for me, I started to suffer terrible anxiety attacks. I had been plagued by these in the past, but hadn't experienced them for many years. Now they came back with a vengeance. I'd wake in the middle of the night in a cold sweat. We'd go out for coffee and, despite being a coffee addict, I couldn't even have a cup because the minute I consumed any caffeine, my heart would start racing. I was all nerves, and my anxiety had a single cause: I just wanted my bro to be all right, and I couldn't understand why he wasn't.

We were to fly back to the UK the day Andrew was booked in for his operation. The doctors had told us there was a very high chance the operation would be a success, and that the cancer would be contained. Michael and I clung to that. We did what we could to stay positive as we said goodbye and boarded our flight.

We had a stopover in Dubai. The flight time from Australia is about thirteen hours, which meant that by the time we touched down in

the Middle East, Andrew's operation was complete. I got on the phone to my dad the moment we stepped off the plane. 'How did the operation go?' I asked him.

Dad sounded a bit quiet. 'Well,' he said, 'they removed what they needed to remove.'

'So it's a success, right?'

'Well ...' Dad replied, 'the thing is, it's spread.'

The moment he said those words, I felt myself thrown into a downward spiral. It was then that I knew that Andrew's

This photo is one of the saddest for me. We really thought he could beat it. We really did.

condition was really, *really* serious. I immediately offered to get on another plane and go straight back to Australia, but Dad said, 'No, let's just see what happens in the next few days. Then we can talk.'

So Michael and I returned to the UK, feeling the absence of our brother on the other side of the world more acutely than ever. Just as I had sensed all those years ago that Andrew had been in a car crash, now I truly felt his pain. I couldn't eat properly. I lost weight. I couldn't sleep. And it wasn't just me. Michael could feel it. Chris could feel it. Danny and Debbie could feel it. Distance meant nothing. One of us was seriously ill, and it affected all the others.

> 'Just as I had sensed all those years ago that Andrew had been in a car crash, now I truly felt his pain. I couldn't eat properly. I lost weight. I couldn't sleep.'

At times like this you need a friend. I had a very good one in Emily. I told her what had happened, and she spoke to her dad. Doctor Ru recommended that I get in touch with an acquaintance of his at the Royal Marsden, which is a specialist cancer hospital in London. I did what he suggested and educated myself about the possibilities that were open to Andrew. Then I got straight on the phone to my brother. 'Andrew,' I said, 'would you and your wife come and stay with me? It'll mean we can keep an eye on you as brothers, and we'll be able to get you treatment at the Royal Marsden, which is one of the leading

Opposite: Me and Andrew. Even when we were separated by thousands of miles, there seemed to be some kind of connection between us.

hospitals in the world.' After all, Andrew was a British citizen. He had the right to be here.

'Really?' he said.

'Of course. And we'll do whatever we need to do to get you looked at as soon as possible.'

He accepted. Before we knew it, Andrew and his wife were making the move over to the UK. The plan, of course, was that they would go back to Australia as soon as he was better.

But that was never to be.

I was excited. We all were. I was going to have my bro living with me, we were going to get him better at the Royal Marsden and we were going to take the pressure off Mum and Dad, who weren't getting any younger. And if – *if* – something started to go wrong, they wouldn't have to see it. They were reluctant to let him go, of course. Even though Andrew was a grown man, he was still their baby, just like we all are. I totally get that – I'm sure that when my kids are grown up, they'll still be my little ones. Mum and Dad pointed out that there are great hospitals in Australia too and they were, after all, his parents. But as brothers, we collectively said to Mum and Dad: let us take the stress away from you. He's going to be fine. When he's better, he'll come back to Australia and you can be with him then.

Andrew and his wife arrived and suddenly the house was buzzing. My brothers were around constantly and for the first time in ages we were able to hang out with Andrew, go for dinners together, chill out at the coffee shop we own up the road from my house. He became a regular part of my life. To make things even better, this was around the time I asked Emily to be my partner. In a weird kind of way, despite Andrew's illness, everything felt like it was slotting into place.

Living with me at that time brought with it certain things most people don't have to think about. One of them was TV cameras. I had started filming a new series of my reality TV show. It was Andrew who first brought up the subject of him being part of it. 'I'd like to tell my story on the show,' he said. 'That way, when I beat this illness, I can encourage millions of others in my situation to fight. I want to be the one standing there telling the story.'

'Are you sure?' I asked him. It had never crossed my mind that he would want to appear on the show.

He was sure. It was a brave decision and a good one. He was great on the show. Everyone got to know him, and saw how close we all were as a family. And it was OK because, like him, we really, truly believed he was going to be OK.

'My brothers were around constantly and for the first time in ages we were able to hang out with Andrew, go for dinners together, chill out at the coffee shop we own up the road from my house. He became a regular part of my life.'

Out of respect for Andrew, I don't want to go into too many details of the treatments he had to endure. All I'll say is this: chemotherapy is tough, not least because it messes with your immune system. As the months passed, however, it was clear to all of us that Andrew was getting better. I can't tell you how happy we were as a family. We were able to ring

On stage, doing what I do best. This was taken at the O2 show that Andrew hoped to come to. It wasn't to be.

Mum and Dad and give them the good news: he's improving day by day, he's looking good, he's eating loads. His life was getting back to normal. He'd come with me to pick up the kids and drop them off. I'd invite the boys round to watch the football in my cinema room, and he'd hang out with them just like he would have done before he became ill. And one day we went to the Royal Marsden for a check-up, and the doctor gave us the news we'd all been longing to hear. 'I can't tell you that you haven't got cancer,' he told Andrew. 'All I can tell you is that we can't find it.'

We were so proud of Andrew that day. We were proud of ourselves as a family, too, for making that decision to bring him over to the UK for treatment. He couldn't officially be classed as being in remission until a certain period of time had passed, but when the doctor gave him the positive news that day, and even started talking about maintenance medication – a treatment every six months just to keep any potential recurrence at bay – we finally felt like we could look to the future. Like we could see past the cancer and start making plans.

Strange though it may sound, Andrew had never seen me perform live. (Neither had my sister, for that matter.) Now that he was on the mend, one of the plans we made was that we should rectify this. I had a show coming up at the O2 in London. It was part of my Up Close and Personal tour, and as gigs go, this was one of the biggest. I was incredibly excited that Andrew and his wife were going to be there, and they were equally thrilled and looking forward to it.

The day of the O2 show approached. But when it was only a couple of days away, Andrew started to feel unwell again. It was a shock because, after his check-up, we had honestly thought that he was getting better. He went to the hospital. The doctors were reassuring. 'You need to stay here,' they told him, 'but don't worry, you'll be out in a couple of days. We're sure you'll be fine to make it to the O2.'

But when the big day arrived, he wasn't well enough. The doctors insisted on keeping him in. I was sent into a spin. 'What's wrong?' I thought. 'I don't understand ... I thought he was getting better ...'

I went on stage that night without the thrill of knowing that my brother was finally in the audience. And the next day, I went to see him.

> 'I went on stage that night without the thrill of knowing that my brother was finally in the audience.'

I arrived at the hospital with Michael. Danny was already there when I walked into Andrew's room. Danny gave me this weird look, and shook his head slightly. I didn't understand. He turned to Andrew and said, 'I'm just going to go with the boys to get a cup of coffee. We'll be straight back.'

But instead of taking us for coffee, he took us into another room and gave us the news we had all been dreading since the first moment we heard Andrew was ill. 'It's spread,' he said. 'There's nothing they can do.'

I stared at him, uncomprehending. 'What do you mean?'

'I mean, it's days or weeks.'

I burst into tears on the spot. Sobbed like a baby. Danny started crying. Michael too. 'I don't understand,' I said through my tears. 'I thought he was getting better.'

All Danny could do was shake his head and say, 'No. It's all over.'

The days that followed are a blur. It hurts to remember them, let alone talk about them or write about them. After Andrew, Chris was the oldest son. It was up to him to call Mum and Dad and tell them they had to come to the UK, immediately. I can't bring myself to think about how they must have felt when they received that call. It was the cruellest blow, after being told that Andrew had been doing so well.

Even when he had that final prognosis, Andrew – and the rest of us – continued to fight. We forced ourselves to believe that, if it had cleared once, it would clear again. We met other people at the Royal Marsden who were going through the same thing, and drew strength from their support and encouragement. In the end, however, there was nothing anybody could do.

It was less than two weeks after the O2 show that Andrew left us. I cannot bring myself to relive that time. But I will say this. There are certain emotions that are unlocked at certain times in your life, and in response to certain events. One of those events is the birth of a child. It's a new experience, impossible to describe to someone who has never experienced that amazing gift, and those tears of joy. Another of these emotions is true grief. I'd lost distant family members before, and of course I'd been sad. But when it's your direct blood – your mother, father, brother, sister or, heaven forbid, your own child – the pain is of a particular type that nobody can understand until they've experienced it for themselves.

I can't write about the funeral, or about the days and weeks that followed. It's still too raw. Even now, I can't bring myself to accept that my brother is no longer with us. I find different ways of dealing with the loss. I push it away. Tell myself it's not real. I force myself to believe that Andrew's back in Australia. I was so used to being away from him for so long, that it's really not such a leap of faith.

But deep down, I know that there is a hole in my life and a hole in my family. The edges of that hole are still ragged and sore. One day, perhaps, those edges will soften up. The hole will always be there, though. It can never be filled.

Out of the
Darkness

'When a life goes, there is some comfort to be
found in the idea that a new life will arrive.'

Out of the Darkness

After we lost Andrew, I went into a complete meltdown.

It wasn't just me. All of us did – my brothers, my sister, my mum and dad. I remember all of us saying, at one point or another: 'Why him? Why couldn't it have been me?' When I said it, I meant it sincerely, but then I'd get angry with myself for having that thought. After all, I had children. Responsibilities.

The truth was that I was heading into a very dark place. Ordinarily, I'm a cheerful, happy-go-lucky person. What you see is what you get. But in the time following Andrew's death, I was a complete mess. I don't think I've ever had clinical depression, but when I was younger I had such terrible anxiety that it really laid me low. I thought all that was behind me, but I found myself going down that path again.

My family was surrounded by kindness. But sometimes, in such situations, kindness is difficult to endure. My brother Danny decided to deal with things by throwing himself back into work at the coffee shop we own. He couldn't stay at home – it would have killed him doing nothing all day. I felt sorry for him: all day long, people would come into the coffee shop and, with all the best intentions, offer their condolences. It meant he was being reminded twenty times a day that he had lost his brother. He would find himself stepping out to the back of the coffee shop and bursting into tears.

Many people do the same thing as Danny in times of mourning and throw themselves into work. Michael did it too – it was the only way he could deal with things. Chris, now the eldest sibling, took on the great responsibility of seeing that Mum and Dad were OK. I, on the other hand, couldn't do anything. I was under contract to ITV for my reality show, but I couldn't bear the thought of going back to it. Fortunately, I was able to put it to one side, for a little bit at least. ITV rang me up and, out of respect for my family, offered to stop filming for a month. I can't tell you how much that meant to me. Not only did they give me a month off, they even pulled a couple of shows that had already been filmed, edited and put in their schedule. They didn't have to do that, but I'm so grateful that they did. Imagine how we would have felt if, two nights after we lost Andrew, an episode was broadcast that had been filmed several weeks previously, showing him alive and well. To see our brother on TV when we were grieving deeply would have been intolerable.

'During that month off from filming, I didn't get better. I got worse. My anxiety was off the scale.'

During that month off from filming, I didn't get better. I got worse. My anxiety was off the scale. It got to the point where, if I was out driving and I heard the sound of sirens, I'd start shaking uncontrollably and would have to pull over. I'd freak out, thinking that maybe an ambulance was arriving to take me to the hospital that I never wanted to see again. I'd start crying with only the slightest provocation, and sometimes with no provocation at all. I was in particular turmoil when the kids came to stay. When I told them that their uncle had passed away, they'd burst into tears, and now I felt the burden of having to appear happy, when inside I was experiencing more pain than I'd ever known.

For some people, a month would be enough time to get your head straight and work out a strategy for how you're going to cope with your bereavement. For me, it wasn't. When my month was up, and I couldn't avoid going back to work, I did the worst thing I could possibly have done: I started to grieve publicly. I remember going to do some radio interviews to promote something – don't ask me what, that time is all a blur. I collapsed on the couch and dissolved into tears. All I could say was that I wanted to stop the interview and go home. I would burst into tears in the middle of filming, so that shooting sessions turned into a complete mess. I hated working, didn't want to talk to anyone and didn't want to do the show any more.

With each day that passed, I descended further into a very dark place. I don't know what hell is like, but I can't imagine it's any worse than what I was feeling. And to make matters even worse, I started pushing away one of the few people who could help me out of that hole. That person was Emily.

We'd only been together a few months. It was supposed to be the honeymoon period, but because of my state of mind it had turned into a nightmare. Emily did her best, but she was met by a brick wall at every turn. She'd cook us a meal, I wouldn't want to eat. She'd suggest we go for a walk, I wouldn't want to put my nose out of the door. She'd offer to talk things over with me, I'd go and chat with my brothers or my mum and dad. I didn't feel like discussing Andrew's death with anyone who wasn't family. I was impossible to be with. Stubborn. Emotional. Unresponsive. Not a good person to be around. Thankfully I didn't turn to alcohol or drugs, but I was in the worst possible place. Every day, I pushed poor Emily further away.

Eventually, she realized she had to tackle the problem head on. She

'To make matters even worse, I started pushing away one of the few people who could help me out of that hole. That person was Emily.'

sat me down and said, 'Peter, I'm getting the impression you don't want me round for a while.'

'I guess you've got two options,' I said. 'Option one, you let me go. Go and do what you have to do. And if I ever get through this hell, and you feel like talking, we can talk. Option two, you stick with me through this.'

She looked at me. 'Well, there's only one option,' she said.

'What do you mean? I've just given you two.'

Emily shook her head. 'No,' she said. 'There's only one option. Of *course* I'm going to stick with you. We're going to ride this out together.'

The moment Emily said that, I knew I'd end up marrying her. This was the time I needed her the most, and she was there for me. And even though I was constantly driving her away, the fact that she had the strength and the urge to fight against me and my stubbornness made me realize she was the one. I was in hell, and if she could put up with me through this, she could put up with me through anything.

I can't say that I 'got over' Andrew's death. I can't even say that I came to terms with it. Finding myself in a position where I could get on with my life was a slow process. I continued to grieve in public. I almost wish I'd disappeared for six months, away from everything, but I couldn't do that. With Emily's help I gradually found the strength to face life without Andrew. But that's not to say I didn't still find things difficult, or that people didn't find *me* difficult. My manager Claire rang me up one day and

'I almost wish I'd disappeared for six months, away from everything, but I couldn't do that. With Emily's help I gradually found the strength to face life without Andrew.'

'"There's only one option. Of course I'm going to stick with you. We're going to ride this out together." The moment Emily said that, I knew I'd end up marrying her.'

said, 'Listen, Pete, I've had a call from the charity Cancer Research UK. They want to know if you'd like to get involved with them in some way.'

My reaction was pretty severe. 'I don't ever want to hear that word again,' I said. 'Not ever. I'm not interested in anything to do with that word. I don't want it mentioned to me. I don't want to see it written down. Tell Cancer Research, I'm sorry, but I don't want to get involved.'

'OK,' Claire said with her usual tact, and she dropped the subject.

It was about a month later that I reached a turning point in my life, and it was thanks to a conversation I had with my brother Mike. I must have been particularly difficult to be with, because he was pretty robust with me: 'Bro,' he said, 'I'm going to tell it to you like this. You'll never get *over* it, so get *on* with it.'

I was momentarily stunned by what he said. He didn't leave it there.

'Bro,' he continued, 'we're *all* hurting. We're *all* going through this pain. What about Mum and Dad? How do you think *they* feel? They're dying inside. They've lost their son. It's not normal. What about Debbie, how do you think *she* feels over in Australia, looking after her little boy and our mum and dad, without us there to help her?'

I admit I grew angry with him. 'It's fine for you to say that,' I snapped. 'You don't know how I'm feeling.'

'Don't you think I'm hurting too?'

'I know,' I said. 'But you don't have to say all this stuff to me.'

'I do. You need to get on with it.'

He was, of course, completely right. The moment I came to terms with the fact that I really wasn't going to get over my brother's death was the moment my life started to get back on track.

'The moment I came to terms with the fact that I really wasn't going to get over my brother's death was the moment my life started to get back on track.'

All of a sudden, I had a change of heart. I suppose I began to realize that I had the support of so many people – my brothers, my sister, Emily and the great British public. And I began to think that maybe, out of this awful, horrible situation, some good could come. So I called Claire and said, 'I want to get involved with Cancer Research.'

She didn't sound surprised. Quite the opposite. 'I thought you would,' she said.

I was very anxious. 'Don't let me down, Claire,' I said, 'because this is going to be hard for me.'

'Maybe,' she agreed. 'But it's going to help you too.'

As usual, she was right.

My first step into the world of raising cancer awareness was a piece I did for *This Morning*, which involved returning to the Royal Marsden hospital. The Royal Marsden is a fantastic place, but anybody who has ever spent a good deal of time there, and then lost someone, will know how difficult it can be to return.

This Morning wanted me to go to the hospital, meet with some of the doctors and surgeons, and discuss their new technology with them. We'd talk about how far cancer research had come, even in the past couple of years, and where it is heading in the future. The piece would run over a week, and I was as nervous as hell. I felt like I was walking back into the fire, and I was going to be live to camera. What if I burst into tears on live TV?

I remember feeling incredibly uncomfortable the moment I walked back into the Royal Marsden. All the old emotions started to well up inside me. But I got stuck in. The doctors and surgeons showed me some of the amazing machines they'd developed for cancer treatment, and opened my eyes to some of the astonishing advances they had made. What they are doing is truly incredible. The more I started listening to them, the more I felt myself getting involved and wanting to know more. And I started to realize that this was about much more than just my brother and our family. This was about *all* cancer patients, and *all* families that might be about to go through what we'd had to endure. It was about finding a way to help people avoid that terrible trauma.

> 'As the week progressed, I felt this incredible drive within me. A drive to do whatever I could to help.'

As the week progressed, I felt this incredible drive within me. A drive to do whatever I could to help. It was almost as if I'd gone on to autopilot. *This Morning* were very happy with the piece and as a result I found myself sitting down with some of the heads of Cancer Research UK to talk about how I might be able to help them in their work.

The charity is like the trunk of a tree, with many different branches growing off it. They wanted me to find my own branch, a way of reaching out and using my position as a person with a profile to encourage people to support Cancer Research UK. They had a brilliant suggestion about how I might do that. The idea was that I should set up the Cancer Research UK Peter Andre Fund to help fund a mobile, on-road unit which forms part of the Cancer Awareness Roadshow. Think in terms of health information and trained nurses on a bus. You don't go to these units for a diagnosis, but they pull up in front of supermarkets or shopping centres and invite members of the public in to check their BMI, or do a breath test if they're smokers to see how much carbon monoxide is in their breath, or have their waist measured. While on board they can ask any questions they might have about the different types of cancer and their symptoms, and be encouraged to think about their body and any unexpected changes they might be experiencing. There are leaflets to take away and the nurses on board can give good, sound advice on healthy living, and encourage you to see a GP if you're worried about something. The Roadshow serves a very important purpose: to make the public more comfortable with the idea of thinking about their bodies, and to be on the lookout for unusual or persistent changes. Because spotting these changes early is the key to increased cancer survival rates.

I'm a guy, and I know how stubborn we guys can be about getting ourselves checked out. I've always been the same – resistant to the very idea of going to the doctor if I've got a cold, or something I don't consider serious enough to warrant a consultation. I like to joke that it's because we've been battered for so long about getting 'man flu', that we've become far too stubborn about getting ourselves down to the GP when we have that sneaking suspicion that something isn't right. But the truth is,

YOUR
HEALTH
CANCER
RESEARCH
UK

REDUCE YOUR
CANCER RISK
DRINK LESS ALCOHOL
EAT HEALTHILY
KEEP A HEALTHY
WEIGHT

I love working for Cancer Research UK, and am a proud ambassador. We know our own body so we need to listen to it.

it's not a joke any more. One person in two is going to be diagnosed with cancer at some point in their life. Think about that: half the population. Do you really want to be part of that half? Even if you're not, chances are that, like me, you're going to be close to someone who is affected by it. Do you, and they, really want to go through that pain?

The core of my message is that early detection is the key to successful cancer treatment. The earlier you catch the illness, the higher your chances of beating it. I am haunted by the thought that if Andrew had got to the doctor earlier, he might still be here today. I know we can sometimes be embarrassed talking about our health issues, but we know our bodies and we often know when something isn't right. I had meningitis once and I *knew* something was deeply wrong, even though everyone around me was telling me that I probably just had flu. So when you have that feeling, get checked out. If you have a mole that changes size or colour, get it looked at. If you have a pain that won't go, speak to a doctor. You could not only potentially be saving your own life, you could be saving the grief of everyone around you. Even if you're reluctant to do it for yourself, do it for them.

The London Roadshow for which Cancer Research UK asked me to raise money is central to spreading this message. To keep it on the road requires a substantial amount of money. I know from my experience with other charity work that people can be very giving in this country, but I wanted to do more than simply ask my fans to donate a fiver or a tenner to this good cause. So we came up with the idea of Pete's Champions, as a way of making people feel more connected and more involved. My Champions raise money for the Fund by organizing events that they themselves enjoy, and I show my appreciation by offering different kinds of thank-you prizes to Champions who raise certain amounts. If you're interested, you can find out more about this on the Pete's Champions section of the Cancer Research UK website. But really, the prizes aren't the main reason my Champions do what they do. They raise money because they know how important this cause is.

Pete's Champions are an amazing bunch, who do great things and raise enormous sums. The Peter Andre Fund raised more than £200,000 in 2015, which goes a long way to keeping the London Cancer Awareness Roadshow on the road. That money has helped give potentially life-saving information to more than thirty thousand people.

And if the money that Pete's Champions raise saves just one life, if it encourages just a single person to get checked out early and so beat this terrible disease that wreaked such havoc on my family and so many others – for me, that's worth everything.

One of my awesome Champs, Christina Cygan, who's raised loads of money for the Fund.

Pete's Champions was created to give people a chance to find innovative ways of raising money for Cancer Research UK. These are just some of my amazing Champions after we'd appeared together on ITV's *Lorraine*.

I know, beyond doubt, that Andrew would be proud of what we're achieving. I also understand that it's now about more than us and our brother. It's about other people and other families. Andrew inspired what we're doing, but it's bigger than that now. And while I know that nothing can bring him back, or fill the hole that his absence has left in my life, it is at least a comfort that something positive has come of his passing.

'I know, beyond doubt, that Andrew would be proud of what we're achieving.'

Emily always makes me
smile with her great sense
of humour.

That because he, and we, went through the pain of a terminal cancer diagnosis, perhaps other people might not have to.

When a life goes, there is some comfort to be found in the idea that a new life will arrive.

I knew by now, beyond doubt, that Emily and I would be together for the rest of our lives. Meeting her had been like meeting an angel. She had helped me through a horrific time, and been by my side as I dragged myself out of a dark, horrible place. She also seemed to be coping well with the more unusual aspects of being with somebody in the public eye. Paparazzi are a fact of life for someone in the entertainment industry. Of course, a lot of people have to cope with them a great deal more than I do, and although they go with the territory when you're in my line of work, I sometimes struggle to understand why the law allows someone to take a photograph and use it however they want. I say this without meaning any disrespect to any of the paparazzi guys, but if you sit in a tree and take a photograph of someone in their bedroom, you're a Peeping Tom. Take a picture of them in the street and you're not. There seems to be no balance. From my perspective, I think the law should be altered so that you can't print a picture of someone without their permission.

Having said that, I have a very good relationship with photographers. It's normally the same guys on the circuit, so we know each other well. We're friendly and have a good mutual understanding. If I don't want to have my picture taken, I can tell them and they normally respect my wishes. I mean, I'm a forty-three-year-old guy, I'm not twenty any more, and we all have those days when we think we don't look so great! Sometimes, if I'm rushing into a theatre to do a show, I'll ask them to

Opposite: Pregnant with our wonderful Amelia.

hold off until after the show, when I'll come out and give them the time they want. Even when they're being more intrusive than I'd like, I try to remember that it's just work for them. Once I was in Cyprus and a big story was brewing. The press were camped outside my house, but it was a boiling hot day and I was worried they'd dehydrate. So I went outside and took them some cold drinks. I think that's the right attitude to have, because when people in my position get their backs up with photographers, that's when they get hounded. Plus, they are generally lovely guys just doing their job.

I can fully understand, though, that if you're not used to that world, it can seem a bit overwhelming. Emily handled it well from the start. In a sense she's lucky because she can choose when she's in the spotlight and when she's not. If I'm invited to an event like the Pride of Britain or the Military Awards, it's up to Emily whether she accompanies me or not. Sometimes, of course, it's out of her hands, and it does occasionally upset her when she's photographed in the street at a time when she's not feeling at her best, or if she has our daughter with her. And she did freak out once when somebody kept trying to photograph her while she was taking her driving test. But in general she is very understanding. She realizes that she has chosen to be with a person who is in the public eye and that there are certain things that come with the territory. She is very good at dealing with it.

When Emily told me, about six months after we had got together as a couple, that she was pregnant, it was one of the most poignant and happiest moments of my life. I'm built for fatherhood. Out of everything I do, being a dad has always come first. The idea of bringing a new baby into the world with Emily was a very special one indeed.

Opposite: Christmas is always a wonderful time for us, but knowing Amelia was on the way made that year extra special.

'We're in the business of saving lives.' HIPZ is an incredible project that is making huge changes to the healthcare system in Zanzibar. Let's keep it going. This picture shows my dear friend Carl, my brother Mike and me outside Makunduchi Hospital.

Opposite: The charity bike ride I did in Zanzibar was nowhere near as flat as it looks in these pictures!

Not long after Emily fell pregnant, I found myself in Zanzibar again. I had promised Ru that I would take part in a charity bike ride, lasting several days, across the island. To be honest, I was pretty scared by the prospect, as I'd never really ridden a bike before, apart from cycling to school. Even in the gym I've always been more of a running-machine man than an exercise-bike man. But Ru talked me into it, telling me that the island of Zanzibar was practically flat. Take it from me: it isn't!

It was still something of a secret that Emily was pregnant, but as I was going to be cycling alongside Ru, taking regular calls from his daughter, I felt I had to tell him. Nobody else on the bike ride knew, however. I was terribly worried about Emily – she was doing her final medical exams and feeling sick because of the pregnancy – and so I was constantly on the phone to her. I think everyone must have thought I was a bit over-keen! It was a strange time. I felt I should have been by Emily's side, but so many people had pledged so much money to HIPZ that I really couldn't let everybody down by not doing the bike ride.

I soon found out that Ru hadn't been entirely honest about Zanzibar being flat. There's nothing quite as demoralizing for a non-cyclist as seeing those hills rise in the distance and knowing you've got to climb

them! My legs were like jelly on the third day. Some days, we would only cycle 20 kilometres. Some days forty. On one particular day we were scheduled to do 60 kilometres. The wind was against us that day, which was horrible. And 60 kilometres turned out to be an under-estimate. Sixty turned to seventy. Seventy to eighty. By the end of the day we'd cycled 90 kilometres through the blazing African heat. I know some of you might be thinking, Don't exaggerate, Pete. But I honestly can't tell you what it was like for a non-cyclist. I've never been so exhausted. Not being much of a water-drinker, I was on the brink of collapse through

Below: Carl, Mike and I were elated – and exhausted! – once we crossed the finish line. But what an achievement.

Opposite: Ru is the founder, hero and heart and soul of HIPZ. In recognition of his services to healthcare, he was awarded the BEM (British Empire Medal) in the 2016 New Year Honours.

dehydration when we reached our destination. I had to be treated with electrolyte-replacing fluids to keep me on my feet. I was certainly no Bradley Wiggins.

Dehydration and jelly-legs aside, we had some great moments on that trip. We met a lot of the locals of Zanzibar, and saw some of the most beautiful scenery. Places unblemished by human habitation, greens of a colour I'd never seen, unspoilt, untouched, unpolluted. A reminder that parts of Zanzibar are a true paradise, and its people some of the nicest I've met. It spurred me on to do more to help the people of that lovely island.

Once Emily had fallen pregnant, I knew that I would ask her to marry me at some point within those nine months. It was clear to us both that our son or daughter would be born out of wedlock, but it was

very important to me that Emily and her parents should know that my commitment to her and to the baby was absolute, before the child was born.

Being a bit of a romantic, I thought long and hard about how, when and where I was going to propose. I had lots of ideas, but none of them seemed quite right. That's not to say I didn't start making plans. On one occasion, we were in Australia, visiting my mum and dad, when we walked past a huge poster of a fantastic, classic engagement ring. Emily stopped in the street to stare at it. 'Oh my God, Peter, look at that!'

I pretended not to be that interested, but later that day I went back to take a picture of it. Back in the UK, my manager Claire's sister put me in touch with a great jeweller, who went about getting the ring replicated. That ring sat in my safe for ages while I tried to think of the best, most romantic way to ask Emily to marry me. Maybe I should take her to Venice or Paris? Maybe we should go up to London and I could pop the question at a fancy restaurant?

Somehow, none of those ideas struck a chord. Time passed, and the perfect moment never felt like it had arrived.

Christmas came and went. We'd been working hard on getting the nursery decorated and kitted out, but Emily still didn't have it the way she wanted it. I suppose we were cutting it a bit fine, since the baby was due on 26 January 2014 – Australia Day. For New Year's Eve, we had been invited to Emily's parents' for dinner. I woke up at home that morning and I suddenly knew, beyond doubt, that today was the day I had to propose. Don't ask me how or why I knew – it was just one of those feelings you can't ignore.

I secretly rang Emily's mum, Rebecca. She knew that I intended to

Opposite: We always try to make Christmas with the kids as special as possible.

EXPRESS MAIL SERVICE

PLEASE DELIVER THE
ENCLOSED PRESENTS TO

JUNIOR

DELIVERY DATE: 25TH DECEMBER

IF UNDELIVERED PLEASE RETURN TO
FATHER CHRISTMAS, THE NORTH POLE

EXPRESS MAIL SERVICE

PLEASE DELIVER THE
ENCLOSED PRESENTS TO

BISTA

DELIVERY DATE: 25TH DECEMBER

IF UNDELIVERED PLEASE RETURN TO
FATHER CHRISTMAS, THE NORTH POLE

propose, but didn't know when or how I was going to do it, because neither did I! I furtively told her that I intended to do it that day. She had a plan. At Emily's family home there is a little lake with an island in the middle. Rebecca suggested that when we came down I should hide the ring on the island, then suggest to Emily that we go for a boat ride and unexpectedly 'find' the ring. I couldn't do it. What if it was raining? What if Emily didn't fancy a boat ride? What if the island was covered with mud, or I couldn't find the ring once I'd hidden it? What if one of the ducks swiped it?

In any case, I was jumping the gun. There was still something else I needed to do before I could pop the question. You've probably got the idea by now that both Emily and I come from very traditional families, albeit very different ones. Just as I had felt obliged to ask Dr Ru for permission to ask Emily out, so it was very important to me to gain his permission to ask her for her hand in marriage. I asked Rebecca for Ru's number at work and, while Emily was in the bath, I called him.

Now, Ru's a busy guy. A surgeon, remember. For all I knew, he might have been preparing to go into theatre. When he picked up the phone, I certainly had the impression that he had people all around him. But this couldn't wait. It had to be now. 'Ru,' I said urgently, keeping my voice down so that Emily wouldn't hear me. 'It's Pete.'

'Oh ... hey, Pete ...'

'Can I ask you something?'

'Um ... look ... can we talk later?' He sounded for all the world as if he were trying to get out of the conversation.

'No,' I said. 'I've got something to ask you. I'm going to do it!'

'Do what?'

Opposite: Baby, it's cold outside! Keeping warm on a skiing trip with Emily.

'I'm going to ask her the question.'

Busy or not, now was the time for Ru's mischievous side to come out. 'What question?' he asked innocently, knowing full well what I was talking about.

I drew a deep breath. 'Ru,' I said, 'do I have your permission to ask your daughter to marry me?'

There was a long pause. Possibly the longest I've ever endured.

Then, he said: 'Course you can, you 'nana. What time are you coming down today?' He said it almost conversationally, as if he couldn't bear the emotion of the moment.

'You're a star!' I said. 'I'll speak to you later.'

I hung up. I had Emily's father's permission. So now there was only one thing left to do. I grabbed the ring, took it into the nursery and placed it on a chair in the centre of the room, with a spotlight shining down on it, making the stone glint beautifully. Then I ran to the bathroom where Emily, wrapped in a towel, had just got out of the bath.

'Sweetheart,' I said, 'there's something I've got to show you in the nursery. It's so funny!'

'What?' she asked. 'Can't I get dressed first?'

'No,' I told her. 'You have to come and see it now. It's the cutest little thing ever.'

Emily had no idea what I was on about as I led her across the hall to the nursery. When we reached the door, I turned her round and brought her in backwards. 'Just wait till you see this,' I said. 'The baby's going to love it!' I wanted to make Emily think I was talking about some kind of finishing touch I'd added to the decor of the nursery, so that when she did see the ring, she'd be even more surprised.

Opposite: Our new addition, and what an utter joy she is. Welcome, Amelia Andréa. Look at the joy in Emily's face. She's such an amazing mum.

We were inside the room. I gently turned her round. There was the ring, the light reflecting off it perfectly.

She stared at it. 'Are you serious?' she breathed.

By now, I was welling up. All I could do was nod and say, 'Yes.'

She broke down. And for nearly an hour, we sat on the nursery floor. Emily was crying with happiness. It was a beautiful moment. And for all my weeks and months of planning different scenarios for my proposal, I knew that here, in our unborn child's nursery as we looked forward to a special new year, was the perfect time and the perfect place for me to ask the woman I loved to marry me.

We made the trip to Emily's mum and dad's house that day. The champagne came out and it was a lovely, happy occasion. I was glad to be able to show Emily and her parents that I was truly committed to their daughter, because I'm not sure Ru thought I was all that serious when I first requested his permission to ask Emily to be my partner. And I knew, with total certainty, that I was marrying the right person. Someone kind and caring. Someone fun. Someone who shared the same interests and passions as me. Someone whom I knew would be an absolutely wonderful mother to our child.

'And I knew, with total certainty, that I was marrying the right person.'

And as it turned out, popping the question on New Year's Eve was a wise decision. Our beautiful daughter Amelia was born three weeks early, just a few days later at Musgrove Park Hospital in Taunton. It was, ironically, the place where Dr Ru had operated on me several years beforehand and it felt like things had come full circle.

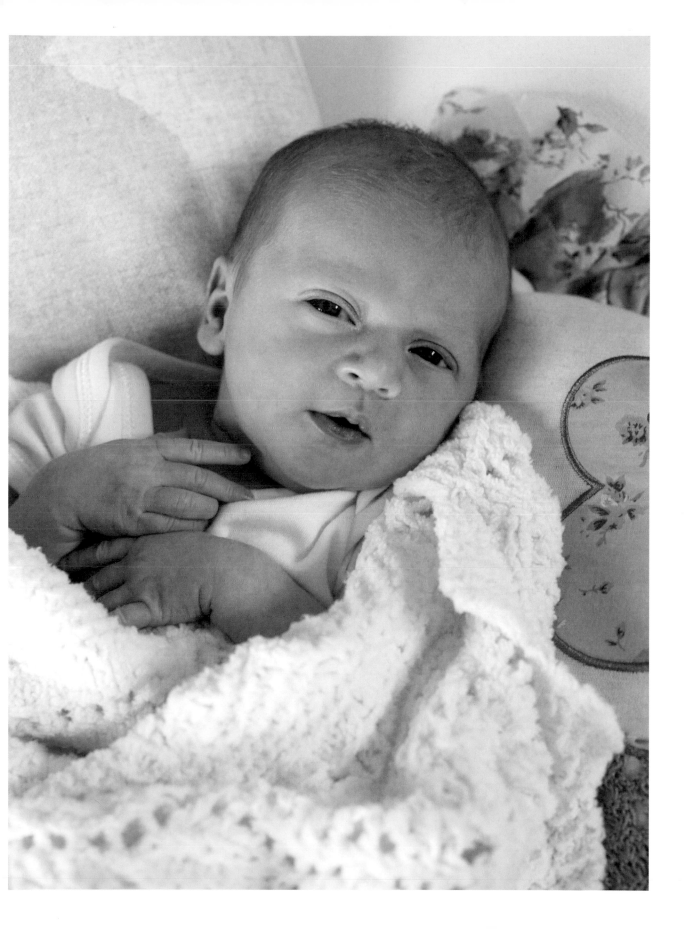

The Wedding

'Emily was by far the most beautiful bride
I'd ever seen, and when she joined me
I could only find one word: "Wow!"'

The Wedding

I didn't think we should get married straight away. We'd got engaged at that particular moment because the baby was soon to be born, and I didn't want Emily to think that we weren't committed to each other. But now that we were engaged, there was no reason to rush the wedding. I was thinking along the lines of two years.

Emily was thinking within a year. But for some reason that thought freaked me out. Maybe it was to do with having recently lost my brother. I think I just wanted to enjoy that happy period of engagement. Marriage lasts for ever, whereas an engagement only lasts for a short time. I wanted to revel in it. To take our time.

I don't know if I was giving Emily the wrong message or not. But every time she looked at a dress, or brought up something to do with the wedding, a little voice in my head would start saying: no, it's too early. It wasn't that I didn't want to get married, or that I wasn't a hundred per cent sure it was going to happen. I just didn't want to rush things.

Emily was fine about the way I felt. But then a call came through from Australia that something had happened to Dad. Now, my dad very seldom gets sick. As I write this he's eighty-three, and I don't think I can really remember him so much as taking a paracetamol. He's one of those supermen, one of those guys you always expect to be OK. For his own privacy, I don't want to go into detail about what happened to him, but suffice to say he had a scare. And that meant we had a scare. So much so that we were a hair's breadth away from jumping on a plane to go to Australia.

It turned out that Dad was going to be fine, but at that moment it dawned on me that, if we delayed the wedding for another year, we would be asking Mum and Dad to wait another twelve months before making the gruelling trip to the UK. At their time of life, and in their state of health, that was a big ask. Dad had just had a health scare out of the blue. What if it happened again? What if one, or both, of them wasn't able to fly?

So I called my dad and I asked him straight up: would you rather we arrange the wedding to happen very soon, or do you want us to wait another year and come to the UK then? He said he'd speak to his doctor. When his doctor gave him the OK to fly, he told us that he'd prefer us to have the wedding sooner rather than later.

I spoke to Emily and asked her if we should bring the wedding forward. She was over the moon. And the way I looked at it, it's much better to bring a wedding forward than push it back, because then someone might start thinking something's wrong! Except, of course, organizing a wedding takes time, and suddenly time was something we didn't have. So when I said, 'How would you feel about getting married in eight weeks' time?' she could hardly believe what I was saying. 'At least with me, nothing's predictable!' I told her.

Once she'd ascertained that I was serious, she rang her family to tell them of the sudden change of plan. 'Let's do it!' they enthused. And so everything was set in motion.

Now, we had big plans for our wedding. Our thoughts were along the lines of an enormous castle with enough space for everybody to stay, fantastic entertainment, brilliant food and a whole load of fun. To pull those plans together in eight weeks was a massive ask for anybody. Fortunately for us, my manager Claire had heard of an amazing wedding planner called Julie Arnold. We rang her, explained what we had in mind and asked her if it was possible to pull something like this off in eight weeks. Julie turned out to be a real superhero, and even when we first gave her an idea of the scope of our plans, she was unflappable. 'If you want it,' she said, 'we'll do it.'

So we did.

'When I said, "How would you feel about getting married in eight weeks' time?" Emily could hardly believe what I was saying. "At least with me, nothing's predictable!" I told her.'

I asked George Nicolaou, my best friend from Australia with whom I'd bonded at school when were both bullied for looking different, to be my best man. George and I have had each other's backs ever since those early days in the playground. He's not just a guy you can totally rely on, though. He's also the kind of bloke you can't help sharing some laughs with, and we'd certainly done that in the past. He's a very important part of my life. So let me tell you about George, and some of the moments we've shared.

Back in the day, when we were in our twenties, I was dating a girl in Los Angeles. It wasn't even remotely serious. Perhaps I should have had second thoughts about hanging out with her when she pointed out a

A slightly heavier me with my greatest friend in the world, George Nicolaou. (You can tell I've given up Heineken now!)

hole in the wall of her house and told me that it was from when she'd had a fight with her previous boyfriend and she'd put a baseball bat through the masonry. She didn't seem too crazy, though, so we carried on dating. I'd gone out there to see her on one occasion, and Georgie had come over to visit me in LA.

I've already told you how much of a buzz I get from that city, so you can imagine how stoked I was that my oldest friend was coming over from Australia. I was desperate to show him the city. We went out one night and saw the sights – nothing more than that, and certainly nothing controversial. We were just two wide-eyed Australian kids in the bright lights of Los Angeles. When we got back to this girl's house, she freaked out. She was absolutely furious that I'd been out having a good time with my old friend, and not with her. I couldn't understand why she was so angry – it wasn't even as if we were in a very serious relationship – but she wouldn't have it. She was effing and blinding and she decided to kick me out of the house.

I suddenly saw a side to her that told me this was not a relationship that was going anywhere. I was happy to leave. 'But I can't just walk out,' I told her. 'All my stuff's here.'

That made her freak out even more. She yelled at me even harder to leave.

'Gladly,' I said. 'I'm out of here. Just let me get my stuff and I'll go.'

She wouldn't listen. Instead of letting me grab my gear, she called the police.

Now, LAPD officers are a pretty hard-bitten bunch. What you see in the movies isn't far from the truth. So there's me and George, two Aussie lads from the Gold Coast, suddenly stranded in LA, sitting on the doorstep of this house, wondering how we're going to get my stuff back, when the cops are suddenly on us. Two LAPD officers, hands on their holsters. *'Step away from the door!'*

'What?!'

'STEP AWAY FROM THE DOOR!'

'Sorry,' I call out. 'I'm confused ... I ...'

'PUT ... YOUR ... HANDS ... UP!'

One thing I knew was this: when an LAPD officer tells you to put your hands up, you put your hands up. I did so immediately. Georgie, however, had a different idea. He stuck his hands into the pockets of his leather jacket. 'I'm not putting my hands up, man. This is injustice!'

'George,' I hissed, 'put your freakin' hands up!'

'Nah, man, in Oz they don't do this ...'

I was terrified. I could see their firearms. They had their hands on them.

'Dude, this is not Australia. These are LAPD. They carry guns, and they use them ...'

'PUT YOUR HANDS UP ... NOW!'

George reluctantly put his arms in the air. The cops approached and immediately handcuffed us, then pushed us against the wall. 'We've heard there's been domestic problems ...'

I took a deep breath. 'Sir,' I said. 'May I call you sir? Please, go inside, take a look round her place. There's a hole in one of her walls and she told me she put it there with a baseball bat during a fight with her ex-boyfriend. So maybe you could check out her police record?'

The cops did what I suggested. Minutes later their attitude had changed and they were uncuffing us. 'You poor, *poor* guy,' one of them said. 'If I were you, I'd get your stuff, leave and never come back.'

All of a sudden, we were getting along brilliantly. I think they loved the idea of a couple of naive Aussies finding themselves in the wrong place at the wrong time. They explained that they'd had to handcuff us because they didn't know what they were walking into, and they soon forgave George's bolshy behaviour. Once I'd got my stuff loaded into my car, and we set out across LA, trying to find a hotel that had a room, they even came along to help us! It had gone from being *The Wire* to *Police Academy*.

We laughed about it later, but it had been touch and go for a moment, and it wasn't the only time George's acute sense of injustice nearly got us into trouble. On another occasion we were driving together to Las Vegas. On the way, we stopped off in a typical Route 66, Bates Motel-type place in a town called Tonopah – true Americana. We were up in our room when we heard a full-on disturbance in a neighbouring room. So we peeked through the keyhole to see an immense guy – twice the size of either of us, and wearing a huge cowboy hat – beating a woman senseless. It was horrible, but also a dangerous situation – I knew without question that this man would be armed.

Georgie's not the kind of guy to let something like that pass, however. 'I'm going in there,' he said.

'No way, dude,' I told him. 'These people have got guns, man. This is America!'

'I don't care. I'm not letting him do that.'

'Listen,' I told him, 'if we go barging in, it'll be no help to that poor woman. We're going to go back to our room, call reception and report what's happening.'

George reluctantly agreed. We phoned reception and they confirmed that they knew what was going on and that the police were on their way. That wasn't good enough for Georgie. Like a regular Crocodile Dundee, he suddenly decided he was going to confront this guy. He burst through the door and on to the scene. I had to literally grab him with two hands and manhandle him back across the corridor and into our own room. 'Listen, dude,' I hissed at him, 'I love you like a brother, but you don't understand that you're in a different part of the world now. This is *not* Australia ...' Happily, the incident got sorted without any more input from us.

There was a casino at the same hotel. The following night we went down and the croupier at the poker table was this elderly man who turned the cards so slowly you could pretty much see what they were. We almost couldn't believe he was for real, and even though we weren't really gamblers, we cleaned up that night. It meant we were fully loaded for when we hit Vegas the following day. Back in our room, George said he wanted to go down the following morning and try his luck at the same poker table before we left. 'Mate,' I warned him, 'if we go down tomorrow, they'll take us to the cleaners.'

George, as enthusiastic as ever, didn't believe me. So we hit the tables again the next morning. There was no sign of the old guy. Instead, there was a female croupier who very much knew what she was doing. Not only did we lose everything we'd won the previous night, we lost everything we'd saved for Vegas too. So we headed to Las Vegas with empty wallets, but a couple more stories to add to our collection.

It's those stories, of course, those shared experiences, as crazy as they are, that bring people close together and solidify friendships. After everything we'd done together, I was so pleased that George could be my best man. When we're together, it's like we're twenty years old again. Ahead of the wedding, he came over with his own children, and it was so lovely to see his kids and my kids playing together, just like we used to do all those years ago.

> 'After everything we'd done together, I was so pleased that George could be my best man. When we're together, it's like we're twenty years old again.'

George made the trip to the UK with my other great friend Dennis, whom we call Shtanko. George and Shtanko are close to my brothers as well, of course, and it was so exciting to know that we were going to have some time to hang out together. And then, of course, there was the business of the stag night.

I've never really been big on stag dos. I don't see the attraction of being cajoled into doing something you might later massively regret! Plus, I'm in my forties now. Those days have passed, and when Emily and I

With my boy at my daytime stag do.
He is certainly one of the lads.

discussed the matter, we decided that, since we knew we were going to have the time of our lives when we were married, we should just keep things tame. The guys *did* try to talk me into dressing as a sumo wrestler for the day – g-string and all – and to have a mini-me sumo wrestler handcuffed to me. I was genuinely up for it, but unfortunately the logistics were too difficult and we couldn't make it work.

We had fun, though. During the day, we went clay-pigeon shooting, go-karting and dune-buggy racing. Best of all, my son Junior came with us. I don't mind admitting that I'm a strict dad, but it's also important to me that my son should be my mate. Some people don't agree. I've had people tell me that you should only be a *dad* to your child, not a friend. My response: you do things *your* way, I'll do them *mine* – and I have won Celebrity Dad of the Year, twice ;-). I want to instil in my children many of the things that my mum and dad instilled in me through my strict, traditional upbringing, but I also want them to feel like they can come and talk to me about things that are worrying them. I want us to be able to hang out, go fishing and do all those father-and-child activities I've always wanted to do. So it was awesome to have Junior along to share the day with me and my old friends.

> '**I don't mind admitting that I'm a strict dad, but it's also important to me that my son should be my mate.**'

I drew the line at the evening event, though, even when Junior begged to be allowed to come. Not that it was particularly wild. We hired out a private room above a nightclub and decked it out like a casino, with proper dealers. A bunch of my cousins and friends came down, and my

brothers were there, of course. Obviously, Andrew's absence was a source of sadness, but we raised a glass to him, and lit a cigar on his behalf. There was a great atmosphere, we all had a lot of fun and we managed to keep a lid on the wilder antics into which stag dos can sometimes descend. I came home that night and slept in my own bed, which suited me just fine.

Emily had the same attitude towards her hen night as I did towards my stag, and simply went out for dinner with a few friends. I told her that if she wanted to go out and party, she should do just that. 'That's the last thing I want,' she replied. For me, it was another reminder of why we are so well suited. We'd much rather just hang out with each other than go searching for a wild time. I truly believe that us both wanting similar things out of life is what will keep us together.

Opposite: It was a fantastic day and I'm so grateful to my friends and family who made it.

Below: My evening stag do (which Junior wasn't allowed to attend!). Friends and family living it up in our own private casino.

Mamhead House in Exeter is a beautiful, Grade I-listed Georgian house with amazing views towards the coast. The perfect place for the perfect wedding.

Emily told me in advance that I was going to love her dress. While I knew she was right, and while I knew how emotional I would be on the day, I wasn't prepared to be quite so astonished at how beautiful she looked. The dress was so classy. So elegant. A mixture of Italian silk and French lace, she'd had it made to her exact specifications, and it showed. It set off her amazing blue eyes, and practically reduced me to tears. Our wedding photos – some of which you can see on these pages – were taken by a good friend of ours called Dan Kennedy, and there is one shot in particular that is very close to my heart. Iconic, almost. It depicts Emily standing at the top of the stairs at Mamhead House, her exquisite gown on full display. Every time I look at it, I'm reminded how lucky I am that she agreed to be my wife.

In addition to the dress, I knew Emily and her mum would have very precise and wonderful ideas about how Emily wanted the wedding to be and how she wanted everything to look. They would make sure that everything on the day was as stunning as the bride. Personally, I like nothing better than to entertain people. So when we were planning the event, I said to her, 'Do you mind if I take care of the entertainment and the food, and you can take care of *everything* else? You can have whatever flowers you want, whatever colours you want, whatever design you want – just let me take care of the entertainment and the food?'

She met me halfway. 'Can we do the food together?'

'OK. But the entertainment? Just trust me.'

With the thumbs-up from Emily, I got started straight away. I explained to Julie, who was helping us plan the wedding, what I had in mind. I

Such an iconic shot.
The most incredibly
stunning bride.

wanted there to be a classical quartet. I wanted African drummers and dancers because of our connection to Zanzibar. I wanted Greek music because of my heritage. I wanted Irish music because of Emily's heritage. I wanted a Mexican Mariachi band, just for fun (and because we've always thought that my brother Mike looks a bit like a Mexican gangster). I wanted great, classy jazz piano while we were eating. Oh, and I wanted my ten-piece soul-funk band for later on in the evening. A lot to ask for? You bet. But we did it.

When the day came, and people started arriving at the beautiful Orangery where the ceremony was to take place, we had a wonderful classical quartet playing while people found their seats. The ceremony itself started to the sound of Schubert's 'Ave Maria'. The pageboys – Junior, Emily's ten-year-old brother Joe and my seven-year-old nephew Savandy – entered first, followed by the flower girls Princess and Amelia. I was pretty emotional seeing my kids walking down that aisle, but George was there with a reassuring squeeze of my shoulder as I tried to hold back the tears.

'I was pretty emotional seeing my kids walking down that aisle, but George was there with a reassuring squeeze of my shoulder.'

Emily's bridesmaids – her friends Ruby, Kelly and Olivia, and my sister Debbie – came next, looking fantastic in long, blush-coloured dresses. And then came Emily, her eyes shimmering, on the arm of Dr Ru. I couldn't help welling up. She looked so gorgeous, and to be surrounded by my family and children as she walked towards me was almost too much. Emily was by far the most beautiful bride I'd ever seen, and when she joined me I could only find one word: 'Wow!'

The ceremony itself was beautiful too, but also a lot of fun. Emily's godmother read two poems, including an adaptation of 'Yes, I'll Marry You, My Dear' by Pam Ayres, in which she cleverly changed some of the references to things that were relevant to my and Emily's life together. My brother Chris gave a reading that was also partially in Greek.

> *Love is a word with many meanings,*
> *Each one of joy and of happy feelings,*
> *Love your family and love your friends,*
> *Love is till the very end.*
>
> *Is there a word that can describe this magic day?*
> *The word is love, I hear you say.*
> *Love is something you cannot lend,*
> *Love is till the very end.*
>
> *Husband and wife and lovers as one,*
> *A new life as partners has just begun,*
> *The love here is true, there's no need to pretend,*
> *Love is till the very end.*
>
> *The bride is so pretty, she shines like the sun,*
> *The hard work has started but so has the fun,*
> *Your friends and your families, their love to you send,*
> *We love you both for ever and ever,*
> *Love is till the very end.*

Our wedding rings were very simple. For Emily a platinum-and-diamond band to match her engagement ring. For me, a simple platinum band. Emily and I couldn't hold back the tears as we exchanged our vows and our rings. We weren't the only ones. There were plenty of tears shed in the congregation too, not least by Junior and Princess. Princess was upset at first because she didn't like to see Emily crying. I had to explain to her that they were tears of happiness, which set her off all over again!

At the end of the ceremony, once Emily and I were pronounced man and wife, two singers and a horn player gave a rendition of 'All You Need Is Love', an idea we borrowed from a scene in the movie *Love Actually*.

As we walked outside, the confetti was thrown, and it was then that

'I do.'

the Mariachi band kicked in. I wanted to avoid that lull you often get at weddings for the hour or so when the photographs are being taken. I figured that some drinks and great hors d'oeuvres would go some way to stopping that period from being too boring, and some lively Mexican music would make the time fly by.

Perhaps the classiest part of the day came when the photos were complete, the Mariachi band had finished and the guests were escorted into the main hall for the sit-down meal. If you've ever been to the Ritz, and heard some really beautiful piano playing drifting through the hotel, chances are you were listening to a friend of mine. I met Ian Gomes when I was at the Ritz in London on one occasion, and discovered that back in the day he used to play for Tony Bennett and Frank Sinatra. We got chatting, and Ian was kind enough to say, 'One day, Peter, it would be a pleasure to work with you.'

I told him that the pleasure would be far more mine than his, and I meant it – Ian Gomes is a legend. As it turned out, however, his wife was a great fan of my reality show. 'If there's anything I can ever do for you,' he said, 'you only have to ask.'

He is such a lovely man, and it's not often you get an offer like that from someone with so much talent, experience and respect in the industry. So I decided to take him up on his offer. I gave him a call. 'Ian, obviously we'd love to pay you, but would you be so kind to join us at our wedding and play for us when the guests are eating, if we get you a grand piano?'

'It would be my honour,' he said, and he wouldn't accept any payment. 'Let it be my wedding gift to you.'

So, as everyone walked into the main hall, which looked fantastic thanks to the incredible designs that Emily, her mum and Julie had created, Ian Gomes was playing the most beautiful music. He continued to play for a good couple of hours while we all ate. Then, just before the speeches, I quietly approached Ian and asked him if he would mind playing one of my favourite old standards, 'Fly Me To The Moon'. He launched into that romantic song, and I started singing along, accompanied by the flute player from the classical quartet. It was a really special moment for me, and I thank Ian and his wife, Sally, from the bottom of my heart for being there and helping me make it happen.

Then came the speeches. George had declared that he wasn't going to prepare a speech – he just wanted it to be from the heart. Like all grooms, I was a bit apprehensive about what he was going to say – and Emily was prepared for the usual best-man shenanigans. But he did me proud, just like I knew, deep down, that my oldest friend would. He told the assembled guests that he could easily tell some funny, slightly embarrassing stories about his old mate. 'But Emily,' he said, 'I've got too much respect for you for that. I just want you to know that I can see he's happy. He's beaming. You've brought so much out in him.' It was a lovely, heartfelt speech which, and for this I'll be ever grateful to George, remained completely respectful to Emily.

Dr Ru was the very opposite to George, in that he had prepared a speech as father of the bride, and was incredibly nervous about what he was going to say. His words will stick with me for ever, though. They put a lump in my throat. He admitted that, had someone told him years ago that his only daughter would end up with me, it probably wouldn't have been quite the way he saw things panning out. But when he met me, and he saw how I am with people, with my family and most importantly with Emily, he couldn't wish for anybody else to be with his

Top: Like father, like daughter. Dr Ru really is a very important person in my life.

Bottom: My groomsmen and page boys. From left to right: George, Tom MacDonagh, Chris, Michael, Junior, me, Savandy, Joe MacDonagh, Danny, Will and Sam MacDonagh.

Our first dance, and the start of our new life.

Top: We threw in a Greek tradition – smashing plates – much to everyone's delight. **Bottom left:** A bit of Greek dancing to get into the mood. **Bottom right:** My best friend and best man, George Nicolaou.

daughter. He welcomed my family into theirs, and there wasn't a dry eye in the house.

Once the speeches were over, the African drumming kicked in to lead everyone into the next hall. Those guys were sensational. They played and danced for a good half hour, and even encouraged the guests to join in and have a go at playing the drums.

Once the African drummers had done their thing, it was time for the Greek music to start. (I told you I wanted the entertainment to be out of this world!) My brother Chris is a phenomenal musician. He plays eleven different instruments, and was a massive influence on me when I was a kid getting into music. He got up and started playing the bouzouki, which is a kind of Greek mandolin. As he played, we had a couple of dancers

I wanted to add an African touch for our Zanzibar connection.

come on and smash plates in the traditional Greek fashion. Before long, we were *all* smashing plates – the adults, the kids, everyone – and dancing all over them. It was probably a massive health and safety hazard, but by that time we were too far down the line of partying to care.

Mindful that we didn't only have a Greek heritage to respect, but also the Irish heritage of Emily's father's side of the family, Chris eventually put down his bouzouki, picked up a fiddle and started a little set of Irish music. We were getting truly multicultural! It's not for me to say whether Greek music or Irish music is more conducive to a fantastic party. All I know is that everyone was having an amazing time (not to mention a few Scotches).

It was about ten o'clock at night by the time the Irish music finished. We

My brother Chris: by far the most talented musician in the family. Chris plays eleven instruments, including the fiddle, on which he played some Irish music in homage to the MacDonaghs' roots.

then asked everyone to step outside: it was time for the firework display. I've often heard people say that you shouldn't waste your money on fireworks, because you're simply sending it up in smoke. But when Julie said, 'Trust me, this is going to be spectacular!' I took the view that, if this was going to be an evening nobody was ever going to forget, it was OK to throw everything at it. When the first couple of fireworks went up, however, I had the distinct feeling that we'd made a big mistake and that this display was going to be like one of those back garden jobs you remember from when you were a kid.

I needn't have worried. It did turn into this absolute spectacular, accompanied by a soundtrack of Vivaldi and Mozart. It was meant to be a display that everyone there would remember for the rest of their lives. I think it was just that.

And as soon as the fireworks finished, my ten-piece funk-soul band kicked off their set. Think Rose Royce, the Commodores, the Jacksons – all the music that meant so much to me growing up and through my career. Halfway through their set, I couldn't resist it. I got up with them and sang a few numbers: 'Uptown Funk' and a little bit of Prince. It was a great way to finish what for me had been the best day ever.

> 'All the entertainment in the world would have meant nothing if we hadn't been surrounded by our families.'

But of course, all the entertainment in the world would have meant nothing if we hadn't been surrounded by our families. It was particularly special for us to have the children with us. Of all the special moments from that day, one will always remain close to my heart. At one point

The fireworks
were sensational.
What a night!

Top: Even at my wedding, I couldn't resist getting up and performing with my ten-piece funk-soul band. *Bottom left and right*: My page boy and Emily's flower girl, Junior and Bista.

during the ceremony, Junior was crying. I asked him why, and he simply said: 'At last!' He'd always wanted me and Emily to get married. And although I'd always made it very clear to him and Princess that they only have one mother and one father, they'd grown to love Emily as a stepmum, and it was heartwarming to see how happy they were on our wedding day.

Our wedding was the most fantastic day of our lives. Like all wedding days, it was over too soon. But at least we had the honeymoon to look forward to.

Having brought the event forward at such short notice, I found I was unable to get out of every bit of work that was booked in for the weeks that followed. Emily had commitments too, as she was to start work in a Surrey hospital soon after our wedding. So, although we wanted to take a two-week honeymoon, we found we had to put that idea on ice and settle for a week.

But what a week. We'd been thinking carefully about where we would go, and one location kept cropping up: the Greek island of Santorini. Everyone had told us how beautiful it was, and when we looked at a few pictures we soon came to the same conclusion. It looked stunning and we decided it was the place for us. What we didn't realize was that my road manager, Carl, had booked, a year beforehand, to go there with his fiancée, in order to propose to her. He'd booked to go on the same day, and even the same flight as us! When we arrived in Santorini, we were literally a stone's throw away from each other. Great minds think alike!

We didn't set off for Santorini immediately. As my family had made the long trip over from Australia to be at our wedding, we wanted to spend a little time with them. What's more, I'd been booked for a couple

of festival appearances that I needed to honour. So it was a week after our wedding that we jetted off to the Greek island for some much-anticipated time as a couple.

We spent the first two nights of our honeymoon in the private penthouse of the Canaves Oia Hotel. After a couple of days there, we chartered a private yacht to take us travelling round the islands. I'm not going to lie: being on honeymoon on a private yacht with the woman I love was one of the most fun and romantic experiences of my life. So idyllic and so perfect that Emily started crying the day we had to leave. And though our proposed two-week honeymoon has yet to materialize, it doesn't matter, because we know we've got the rest of our lives together.

Our honeymoon on the beautiful Greek island of Santorini was pure bliss.

Giving Back

'Some people, through no fault of their own,
have been dealt a very different hand to
mine. When you've received a lot, you have to
remember to give something back.'

Giving Back

I've been very lucky in my life. I've had, and have, a great career. I have an amazing family, beautiful children and I've married the love of my life. Of course there have been ups and downs, but barely a day passes when I don't remind myself how lucky I am.

Some people are not so fortunate. Some people, through no fault of their own, have been dealt a very different hand to mine. It's always been in my nature to feel an overwhelming compulsion to help such people. That's why charitable activities are at the very core of what I do and who I am. When you've received a lot, you have to remember to give something back.

I've already mentioned my involvement with HIPZ – Health Improvement Project Zanzibar. When I first travelled to Zanzibar with Dr Ru back in 2012, I felt that familiar compulsion to help, and I can now say quite sincerely that working with HIPZ is one of the most rewarding parts of my career. That's not to say it can't be difficult. People in the UK are generally very charitable and very giving. Sometimes, though, they struggle to understand why we should be raising money for a problem in a far-off place, when there are countless causes in the UK that need supporting.

I have two answers to that. Firstly, I don't believe anyone would go to those hospitals in Zanzibar, and see what I've seen, without being moved

'That's why charitable activities are at the very core of what I do and who I am.'

to help. You can't look at a ward of dead and dying children without feeling the urge to do something about it. You can't look at sick people lying on the dusty ground outside a hospital so poorly equipped that it wouldn't even be worthy of the name in a developed country, without understanding quite clearly that things have to change. Not everyone will have the opportunity to go to Zanzibar as I have, but if I can help by raising some kind of awareness, it can only be a good thing.

Secondly, it's not as if we're talking about raising countless millions of pounds. In Zanzibar, a small amount of money goes a very long way. If HIPZ manages to raise £100,000 a year, that sum will completely cover its annual needs. That £100,000 doesn't simply buy a few tanks of oxygen, or a supply of clean dressings. That money saves thousands upon thousands of lives. As I write this, the hospital I visited has just performed its first caesarean section carried out solely by Zanzibarian doctors. Those doctors have been trained by British HIPZ doctors. Now that knowledge and expertise have been shared, they have it in their power to perform this crucial, life-saving operation, and also to teach others how to do it. I find it incredibly fulfilling contributing to a cause that makes such a massive difference, though of course my contribution is minimal compared to that of others. Dr Ru, for example, works full time as a consultant urologist here in the UK, and spends all his spare time working on the Zanzibar project. That's why, if I can help by being an ambassador for such a worthy cause, I'm very proud to do it.

One of the great advantages of being in a position such as mine, is that I can devote my time to a wide variety of great causes. Another that is very dear to me is the charity Born Free, for which I am also a proud patron.

A respect for wild creatures has always been central to who I am. It's hardly surprising, I suppose, given that I was brought up in Australia. I've already told you how my brother Andrew, being the great animal-lover that he was, really stoked our enthusiasm for the wonders of the natural world. Living in Australia, though, also meant that all my siblings and I were exposed to some amazing – and frankly pretty scary – creatures. Of the ten deadliest snakes in the world, nine live in Australia. With the exception of the Brown Recluse, all the deadliest spiders are indigenous to Oz. I regularly encountered these things growing up. I remember being about thirteen years old and at school. Some kids were shouting at the rest of us, 'Come and have a look at this!' We all formed a circle around this massive funnel-web spider. Now, most spiders, surrounded by a bunch of noisy thirteen-year-old boys, would try to scurry away. Not the funnel-web. It lifted its two front legs, bared its fangs and started hissing at us. This thing was *huge*. A few of the boys – us kids being idiots at the time – tried to step on it. We were lucky none of us made the wrong move. A funnel-web's fangs are easily sharp enough to penetrate soft shoes. If that spider had bitten one of us, we'd have needed to go straight to hospital to get the anti-venom, or we'd have been dead.

On another occasion, my siblings and I were at the house of one of our uncles. My sister had stepped outside for a moment. As she came back in, she stopped and gasped. A red-bellied black snake was coiled up in the groove of the threshold. She was inches away from stepping on it. If she had, it would definitely have bitten her.

The bite of the red-bellied black snake is enough to put you in hospital, but it probably won't kill you. The same can't be said of the various sea snakes that you might be unlucky enough to encounter, as we did one day.

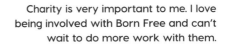

Charity is very important to me. I love being involved with Born Free and can't wait to do more work with them.

'We froze, just in time to see this absolutely enormous sea snake glide past us through the clear water. Sea snakes like that are among the deadliest creatures of all. If one of those bad boys bites you, you're dead unless you get the anti-venom within fifteen minutes, which isn't going to happen if you're on the beach. '

Mum and Dad used to take us to a stunning beach in Coolangatta on the Gold Coast – very close to where I would later film *I'm a Celebrity, Get Me Out of Here!* We used to go up there most Sundays, and it really was an idyllic place to be. One day, however, we were all in the water when Dad shouted, at the top of his voice: *'Don't move! Don't move!'* We froze, just in time to see this absolutely enormous sea snake glide past us through the clear water. Sea snakes like that are among the deadliest creatures of all. If one of those bad boys bites you, you're dead unless you get the anti-venom within fifteen minutes, which isn't going to happen if you're on the beach. Fortunately, the sea snake wasn't aggressive. Dad told us to get out of the water, and our trips to that beautiful beach became less frequent after that.

Swimming in the sea in Australia can be a risky business for all sorts of other reasons too. There's a beach on the north coast near Cairns where you can't swim because the sea is full of saltwater crocodiles – the most aggressive, deadliest type there is. But perhaps even scarier than the

A quiet moment of reflection at the Cynthia Moss Amboseli Elephant Research Project in Kenya. The time I've spent in Kenya, witnessing animals living free, has provided some of the most special moments in my life.

sea snakes and the crocs is a tiny little creature that very nearly killed my cousin Leo. He and my brother Michael had gone swimming near Cairns. They were in the water when Leo said to Michael, 'Bro, I feel like something's bitten me on my back, like a mosquito.'

Michael had a look. 'Yeah,' he said. 'There's something small there – maybe a midgie.'

It was no midgie. A couple of minutes later Leo said that he was really not feeling good. They started walking out of the water, when suddenly Leo collapsed, foaming at the mouth. Michael screamed for people to come and help. A few guys grabbed Leo and quickly rushed him to hospital.

> 'Suddenly Leo collapsed, foaming at the mouth. Michael screamed for people to come and help. A few guys grabbed Leo and quickly rushed him to hospital.'

It turned out that Leo had been stung by what is colloquially called a stinger. Its real name is the Irukandji jellyfish. The Irukandji's body is no bigger than my baby fingernail, though its tail can be up to a metre long. It is transparent, so almost impossible to see in the water. Not only is the Irukandji the smallest box jellyfish in the world, it is also the most venomous. It causes what is known as Irukandji syndrome, the symptoms of which include extreme pain in the back and kidneys, muscle cramps and vomiting. My cousin later said it felt like stampeding elephants trampling on his back. He was barely able to breathe. In the hospital, he was with two guys, one on either side, both of whom had been stung by these jellyfish. The guy on Leo's right died.

Now, I don't want to scare anybody off going to Australia! I have plenty of cousins out there who say they've never seen anything as scary as the wildlife I've just told you about. And in general, the beaches are safe so long as you swim between the safety flags, under the watchful eye of the Baywatch-type lifeguards. The point I want to make is this: I grew up *respecting* wildlife. But the wildlife I encountered was surrounded by human habitation. And there is a difference between respecting wildlife and truly *understanding* it. To understand animals, you have to see them in their natural environment, away from built-up areas and the interference of humans.

'There is a difference between respecting wildlife and truly *understanding* it. To understand animals, you have to see them in their natural environment, away from built-up areas and the interference of humans.'

I have been lucky enough to do this on a number of occasions. The first was in 2008 when I travelled to a game reserve called Thornybush (no giggling at the back) in South Africa. This was nothing to do with Born Free, but was perhaps the moment my deep love of Africa started. In order to get to this park, you have to travel on a tiny plane that lands on a runway right in the middle of the bush. Once you're on the ground, though, you can't simply climb out of the plane and walk freely to a nearby car, because you're so far into the heart of the wilderness that it's perfectly possible a lion will emerge from somewhere and rush you. So, an armed guard has to escort you to your vehicle.

It was a surreal experience. But also wonderful. I don't know what the Garden of Eden looked like, but I imagine it was something like this. I felt like I'd stepped back thousands of years, to a time when humans had barely touched the earth. There was something quite magical about seeing lions and other big cats existing alongside giraffes, elephants, zebras and all the other animals I saw on that trip.

I remember pointing across a particularly spectacular stretch of the savannah and saying to my guide, 'Do people ever go in that direction?'

My guide shook his head quite emphatically. 'No,' he said. 'That's the animals' land. No human has ever been there.'

It was awe-inspiring, looking out on parts of the earth where man has never stood. Maybe it was my imagination, but the grass was a brighter green than I had ever seen, the colour of the trees was more vibrant and there was a sense of peace all around that I'd never experienced.

'I felt like my eyes had been opened on that trip. I'd seen animals up close before, but only ever in captivity.'

I felt like my eyes had been opened on that trip. I'd seen animals up close before, but only ever in captivity. Like lots of people, I've been to zoos and circuses, and so have my kids. I'm not here to dissuade people from going to the zoo, but I will say this: once you've seen these magnificent animals in their natural environment, you begin to have an

Opposite: Growing up in Australia, I've always had a real love and respect for wild animals, which I hope to instil in my kids.

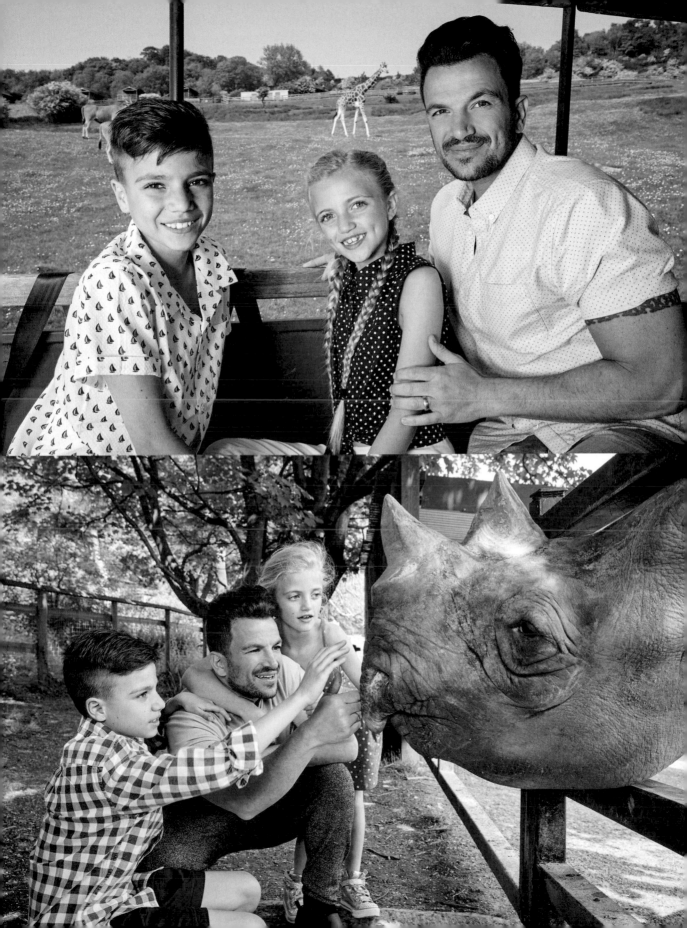

understanding of how depressing it must be for them to live out their lives trapped within four caged walls. I remember being back at the lodge where we were staying, looking out over this vast scenery in front of me, knowing that a leopard could emerge at any moment, and coming to a sudden realization: animals should be *born* free, they should *live* free and they should *die* free.

This was the reason why I first became involved with the Born Free Foundation. It was formed over thirty years ago by the actors Bill Travers and Virginia McKenna, who had starred in the 1966 film *Born Free*. That film was based on the real-life story of Joy and George Adamson, who raised an orphaned lion cub and then released it into the wild. The primary objectives of the Born Free Foundation are to protect species in the wild, and to rescue vulnerable animals from miserable lives in tiny cages.

When I think of caged animals, I can't help wondering how awful a human's life would be if they were forced to live out their days in what is effectively a prison, with people pointing at them and feeding them through the bars of a cage. Perhaps it sounds silly, equating animals to humans like that, but I'm not so sure. You only have to watch the YouTube clip of Christian the lion, who was bought from Harrods and raised by humans who subsequently released him into the wild, much like Joy and George Adamson did. When his former owners went back to find him years later, convinced that he would have forgotten them, the lion greeted them like the surrogate parents they were, jumping on them gently and hugging them. To me, that shows that animals' emotions and needs aren't so far from human ones. We do the natural world a terrible disservice if we fail to respect that.

I'm very proud to be a Born Free patron, and the Foundation has been responsible for some of my most memorable moments over the past few years. In July 2015, I visited Kenya so I could see for myself the amazing conservation work that the charity is doing to stop the decline of the wild lion population in that country. I travelled 150 miles south of Nairobi in an open-top Land Rover to the Amboseli National Park. Here, I learned that the threat to the lions does not only come from hunting. Local farmers lose their livestock to wild animals, and shoot lions in retaliation. I saw how Born Free is helping to solve this problem by building 'bomas' – enclosure fences – to protect the farmers' livestock and encourage the lions to move away from the villages to find their food. The construction of these lion bomas are a small but effective conservation measure, and is going a long way to protecting this species whose numbers are declining steadily and becoming worryingly close to extinction.

I'm pleased to be able to raise awareness of the plight of these animals because I've had the opportunity to see them up close. Maggie and Sonja are two lioness sisters who lived in cramped and squalid conditions in a circus. Thanks to Born Free, they have been re-housed in the Shamwari Game Reserve near Port Elizabeth, South Africa. It was my privilege to meet these lions before they were flown to their new home. When I encountered them at Heathrow Airport, they had travelled by Eurostar from an animal rescue centre in Belgium, and were about to be loaded on to a Dreamliner aircraft that would take them to South Africa. They were caged at the time, of course, but this was to be their last journey before they were finally set free. I was so in awe of those animals. As I approached the cage, one of them roared. It was terrifying and awe-inspiring at the same time. I moved nearer to the cage and talked to her. It sounds silly, I know, but I tried to explain to the lion that she was soon going to be free. It was very humbling, knowing that I was one of the last humans who would ever get up close to her, before she was finally released into the wild where she was supposed to be.

I've met other animals too – gorillas and tigers and all kinds of wildlife – some in the UK, some in Africa. It's amazing how those that have been brought up around humans are strangely humanized. They don't seem to fear us. What they really fear is enclosure. In that respect, they're not so different from us, and that's why I do what I can to help the amazing charity that is the Born Free Foundation.

'I tried to explain to the lion that she was soon going to be free. It was very humbling, knowing that I was one of the last humans who would ever get up close to her, before she was finally released into the wild where she was supposed to be.'

I was in my twenties when somebody recommended that I read a particular book. 'Sure,' I said. 'What's it about?'

'Well,' my friend told me, 'it's about one of the worst cases of child abuse in American history.'

'What? Why would I want to read something like *that*?'

'Trust me,' said my friend. 'It's an unbelievable book. You've *got* to read it.'

So I gave it a go. And once I started reading it, I simply couldn't put it down. The book was *A Child Called It* by Dave Pelzer. It describes how, between the ages of four and twelve, the author suffered sickeningly severe abuse at the hands of his mother. He was starved. He was forced to drink bleach. He was stabbed in the stomach. He was burned and made to eat his own vomit. Eventually, his teachers put a stop to the abuse

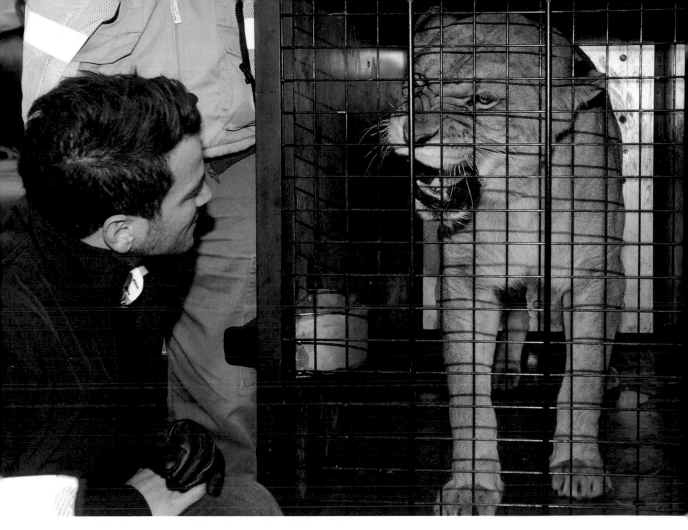

I'm in absolute awe as this amazing beast says her final farewell before she is freed into the wild after years of captivity.

and Dave Pelzer was put into foster care. One of the most astonishing aspects of his story was that, as an adult, he found it in his heart to forgive his abuser. It is a truly remarkable book.

I read *A Child Called It* long before I had children of my own but even so, once I'd read it, I felt my usual compulsion to help when I hear about a cause that really touches me. I had the benefit of a very secure and loving upbringing. The idea that there were children out there who might be enduring even a fraction of what I'd read about in that book was completely horrific to me. I even went so far as to write to Dave Pelzer himself, asking him if there was anything I could do to help other people in his position. I never heard back – I guess he must have been inundated by similar offers – but I simply couldn't get his story out of my head.

Years later, when I was asked to go into the jungle for *I'm a Celebrity, Get Me Out of Here!*, I needed to nominate a charity for some of my fee to go to. I wasn't affiliated with any charities at the time, but that terrible story of child cruelty had not left my mind. So I said I would like the money to go to a charity that helped children in similar situations. That was when somebody explained to me about the NSPCC.

The NSPCC works with thousands of children and families a year. Over the 130 years that it has been in existence, it has protected millions of children from abuse and neglect. Everything they do is centred around the children. Their philosophy is that we can only put an end to child cruelty by listening to children and looking at the world from their perspective. They put children first. This is entirely in accordance with my own view of the world. As a father, I have no greater fear than of something happening to my children, and it appals me to know that there are kids out there who are suffering in silence and are too afraid to speak out.

One of the NSPCC's greatest achievements, in my opinion, is the ChildLine service originally championed by the lovely Dame Esther Rantzen. When I was young, if a child was in difficulty it was almost impossible for them to find someone to talk to. They certainly couldn't phone anybody, because the only phone that they would have had access to would have been the one owned by their mum and dad. If they were being abused by their parents, there was no way they would ever have been allowed access to that phone. With the introduction of ChildLine, children in distress could make a free, anonymous call from a public telephone. It's no exaggeration to say that through that service alone, ChildLine has rescued countless children.

I felt completely compelled to help with the NSPCC, and am a proud ambassador.

Nowadays, of course, kids have much easier access to mobile phones. That doesn't mean that ChildLine is redundant. ChildLine carries out nearly 300,000 in-depth counselling sessions with children and young adults a year, thanks to the incredible dedication of almost 1,400 trained volunteers. It is massive and important work. I think back to my own childhood. Our family was close-knit and loving, but there's no doubt that I had a very tough time of it at school. What I had to endure at the hands of those playground bullies who picked on me for the way I looked is of course nothing compared to what some kids have to go through. But it did make me feel desperate and lonely at times. I didn't want to go to the teachers, because I'd have been branded a 'sneak'. I didn't want to go to my parents, because I was afraid they'd go to the teachers. So I think I would probably have used ChildLine myself, if it had been around in my day.

Having raised a decent amount for the NSPCC from *I'm a Celebrity, Get Me Out of Here!*, the charity asked me if I would like to become an ambassador for them. I did so, and proudly. And when my own kids came along, and I started to understand more about how vulnerable children are and how much support they need from a secure and loving family, my association with the charity became even more important to me. I have supported campaigns such as Now I Know, which aims to teach children and young people greater awareness about child abuse. We want children to be able to say 'Now I know', not 'I wish I had known'. The campaign is part of the Speak Out Stay Safe programme, which is delivered into classrooms by trained staff and volunteers. In 2014, that campaign raised more than £4 million, and I'm very proud to have done my bit in raising awareness of this essential work.

There remains a lot to do. There are still many children out there who suffer in silence, and they don't have to. I hope that, in my own small way, I am contributing to a snowball effect: the more we can stop children from being scared to speak up, the more potential abusers will understand that there's a good chance they'll be found out, and the less abuse will happen. I want to help the NSPCC in their goal to make abusers realize that they can't get away with it. This help is something I believe every adult owes to every child.

There are, of course, children who are not being mistreated but who still need help. And there are smaller charities than the NSPCC who need help raising awareness about the amazing work that they do. Caudwell Children is one of these. It was founded by the businessman and philanthropist John Caudwell, the owner of Phones 4u. Its aim is to help disabled and desperately ill children lead as normal a life as possible. This is a big job. There are approximately 770,000 disabled children in the UK. About 400,000 of those live in, or on the margins of, poverty. They are extraordinary people who need help to live ordinary lives.

Caudwell Children does this in many ways, one of which I find particularly inspiring. If you are a disabled child, you face many different challenges. Perhaps the most pressing is mobility. There is a wide range of very advanced wheelchairs available, but they are expensive and there can be long waiting lists to get access to them on the NHS. Caudwell Children helps families in need get hold of this equipment, some of which is truly remarkable. I've seen powered wheelchairs which, at the press of a button, turn a disabled child into something

Running the London Marathon was a great achievement. More importantly, I managed to raise some money for the NSPCC.

Emily and me at the Caudwell Children Butterfly Ball.

like a Transformer – raising them up so they are at the same height as their peers, and even helping them to walk. It's impossible to overstate what something like this does for the confidence of a child, or how dramatically it improves their quality of life.

Caudwell Children also recognizes the importance of helping the families of disabled children. This is something that is very important, and which often gets forgotten. Caring for a disabled child is extremely hard work. If the children's families don't get sufficient respite, they can become drained of energy and can't focus on their child. Caudwell Children offers short breaks for young disabled people so that they can meet new people and learn to be a little more independent, while their parents and carers can have short periods of well-earned and essential rest.

I've met many amazing children through my association with this charity, and I've been proud to be part of some of the work that it is doing. Every penny that is raised goes directly to where it's needed, and since the charity started in the year 2000, it has raised over £30 million for the children and their families. It's a very good cause, and a very humbling experience to be connected with it, as it is with all the other charities that I support. I take my association with these organizations very seriously, and am proud to raise both money and awareness for these great causes.

'Every penny that is raised goes directly to where it's needed, and since the charity started in the year 2000, it has raised over £30 million for the children and their families.'

Strictly and Beyond

'Maybe it would be a bit of fun. Maybe it would be good experience … So I said yes.'

Strictly and Beyond

My reality show was a central part of my life for a decade. I remember getting to the fifth series and saying: if we ever get to series ten, we'll call it a day. In truth, I'm not sure I ever really thought we'd get that far. But we did, and it was still one of ITV's highest-rating reality shows.

That show documented some of the best moments of my life. Taking the kids to Dubai for the first time, where we stayed in the Atlantis hotel, visited the water park and just had the most brilliant time. Or fishing on the Great Barrier Reef, where Junior caught his first coral trout and his first red emperor. In many ways, it was like having a really high-quality, high-definition home video. It also documented some incredibly poignant moments. We met a lot of people along the way, as the cameras followed our charity work, whose stories were inspiring if sometimes tragic. We met terminally ill patients, and individuals whose refusal to let life get them down was truly humbling. We showed the highs and lows of life.

I think the reason people liked our show was because it really was reality. What you saw was what you got. The crew used to be with us for four or five hours a day, four days a week, but things weren't particularly pre-planned. They really were just following me around as I went about my daily life. We were obviously doing something right, because the audiences kept tuning in. So why would I want to step away from such a high-rating show? What kind of idiot would do that?! Well, there was method to my madness. If you are getting your highest ratings at series ten, chances are that you'll keep those high ratings for series eleven, maybe even series twelve. But at some point, those ratings are going to drop. And when your ratings fall on a reality show – which is all about you – chances are that your other work is going to cool off too, because it means people are getting bored of you!

I took my inspiration from *The Osbournes*, who made the decision to quit while they were ahead. And it turned out to be a great move, because since I called time on the reality show, my other work has been off the scale. Some people ask if I regret stopping the show. I don't, but perhaps that's because I know there's a chance I might revisit it in the future. I certainly will if Junior and Princess have their way! They're forever asking when the cameras are coming round again. For them, it was just part of normal life – no different to the way most kids see their mum and dad going around with a camcorder. It was a very positive experience for them, I hope, and for all of us. I've heard people say that they think Emily encouraged me not to do the show any more, because she didn't want Amelia to appear in it. But that couldn't be further from the truth. I'd already made my decision long before our daughter came

'Some people ask if I regret stopping the show. I don't, but perhaps that's because I know there's a chance I might revisit it in the future. I certainly will if Junior and Princess have their way!'

along. In fact, if I had to pinpoint it to a particular event, I'd have to say that my brother's death was a contributing factor. I was so proud of him when he said that he wanted to appear on the show, to be the one who showed other families going through the same thing as us that it is possible to survive such illnesses. When that didn't go right, it made me wonder how much I wanted to continue.

So, while I may well revisit my reality show in the future, in the last couple of years my TV output has featured a wide range of other genres, including perhaps the best-loved show there is: *Strictly Come Dancing*.

I'd been receiving requests to appear on *Strictly* for a good four or five years. I knew it was a great entertainment show – perhaps the greatest – but there were always good reasons for declining. For a start, I had my reality show, and the commitment and devotion I had to give to that was full on. Secondly, I didn't want not to be good at it! And thirdly, I knew that, although I rated myself as a performer, and was quite comfortable dancing in front of massive crowds, I knew that I was not a *technical* dancer of the type you needed to be, so far as I could tell, to do well on the show. Long story short: I didn't think I'd be all that great on *Strictly*.

But now the reality show had come to an end, the *Strictly* people made another approach and my wonderful manager Claire said: 'I really think this could be good for you.' Up until that point, I'd only really been exposed to an ITV audience. And while ITV are like family, Claire thought it would be a good idea for me to be seen on the BBC. I'd been associated with *Children in Need* with them a few times, but that was about it. Moreover, it would help me promote my current album, *Come Fly With Me* – about which, more later.

So we met with some representatives from the show and they were still very keen for me to be involved. I explained to them my worries. I grew up watching Michael Jackson, Prince and James Brown dancing. When I

For me, in the past, holidays were all about the sunshine but Emily and I both love the buzz we get from going skiing.

go out on stage, I try to emulate what they did, but make it my own. I'm not trained, though, and I'm not technically accomplished.

'Don't worry about that,' they said. 'We've seen you move, we know what you can do.'

OK, I thought. Maybe it would be a bit of fun. Maybe it would be good experience. I'd certainly learn something that could be useful in the future. So I said yes.

Respect to Emily. I don't suppose that she particularly relished the idea of seeing me on national TV dancing with another woman, but she was incredibly cool about me doing the show and completely supported me. She even had an opinion about who I should be paired up with. 'There's this great dancer,' she said, 'called Janette Manrara. You'd be fantastic with her.'

I had no idea who would be on the show alongside me. You just have to say yes or no, without any prior knowledge of who else you'll be pitting your skills against. When the other contestants were announced, I didn't know many of them very well. I certainly had no idea how many of them were any good on the dance floor. I was a little bit alarmed, though, when the bookies put me as favourite to win. It was flattering, of course, that people thought I might be good at it, but the pressure on me to perform well was suddenly massive, and I didn't like that one little bit. I was worried about my lack of technical ability and very aware that none of those people who were predicting I would win had actually ever seen me perform ballroom dancing before.

Emily was clearly in tune with the people choosing the dance partners. I was paired up on day one with Janette Manrara, who I thought was completely awesome. I'm quite short for a guy – just 5 foot 9 compared to

Opposite: We try to go skiing as a family once a year – even the kids are becoming obsessed with it!

some of the other male contestants who were over 6 foot – so I needed someone who matched me in stature. Janette was the perfect person in that respect, but we also got on incredibly well from the very start.

I'll be honest. I didn't really understand quite how gruelling *Strictly* would be. I thought it would be a few hours of rehearsals here and there. In reality, we were rehearsing six to eight hours a day, five days a week. Then we'd perform on the Saturday. The Sunday night show is pre-recorded late on Saturday night, which means that Sunday is your only day off – and by then you'd be wrecked on account of all the work you'd put in over the previous week. I was promoting my latest album and tour too. On top of all that, I also had a house full of kids that I needed to get home to – so, as you can imagine, life was pretty full-on. However, I'm not afraid of a bit of hard work! I'm much more concerned about being underprepared.

'It was flattering, of course, that people thought I might be good at it, but the pressure on me to perform well was suddenly massive, and I didn't like that one little bit.'

When I'm getting ready for a show, three weeks is the magic number. That's how long it takes on tour, for example, for me to feel completely comfortable with my routines. Often, I don't get three weeks' rehearsal time, so I find that it takes a few nights of the tour for the show to bed in. By the time I reach the end of the tour, I'm almost on autopilot. I know every single move instinctively. Luckily for me, we had three weeks' rehearsal time between being paired off with our partners and the first night of *Strictly Come Dancing*. Give me three weeks and I'll learn anything, even a cha-cha-cha, our first dance, which we performed to 'Ain't No Other Man' by Christina Aguilera.

I had a lot of fun getting to grips with that routine. It was my kind of dance. As I was learning, I started to understand what John Travolta had been doing in the movie *Grease*. Since I love John Travolta, I had a blast. When the time came, three weeks later, to perform it live, I felt pretty confident. The response from the judges was overwhelming. Len Goodman said it was the best dance of the opening two nights. One show in, and I was top of the leader board.

Thankfully, it wasn't just the judges who liked what I was doing. I remember them showing *Strictly* on the show *Gogglebox*, where members of the public are filmed watching the TV and giving their – often quite forthright – opinions of what they're watching. One couple observed that the only person they recognized on this series of *Strictly* was me. When, at the start of my cha-cha-cha routine, I had to do a bit of acting, one of them said that we contestants usually acted because we didn't know how to dance. When I started dancing, though, they graciously changed their opinion.

The odds on me winning the series grew even shorter after that first performance. I was way out in front. But I was also way more scared. I flatter myself that I know my strengths and weaknesses. I'd had three weeks to practise that first dance. And if I had three weeks to rehearse for every dance, maybe I'd have been OK. It's not like that, though. For the next performance, I only had four days to prepare. You rehearse Monday to Thursday, then on Friday there's no practising allowed – just a couple of run-throughs on stage, ready for the Saturday performance. I knew I was going to struggle.

Janette Manrara and her fiancé Aljaz have become very good friends with Emily and me since *Strictly*.

My next dance was the quickstep, set to the Zutons' 'Valerie'. I really started to feel the pressure. I felt sick and increasingly worried. I couldn't quite pick it up as quickly as I needed to, and all those technical aspects of dancing that I'd been concerned about proved to be as difficult as I'd imagined. Your shoulders have to be back, but not up. Your neck has to be long, but not forward. Your arms have to be in a position where they can't drop at any time. You have to stand differently to how you normally stand. You have to walk on your toes rather than your heels. And just when you've got used to one particular style of dancing, you suddenly have to switch to a completely different technique. I knew that, eventually, I was going to get into trouble.

Somehow, I managed to get through the next few weeks with reasonably high marks. But I was stressing out badly. I used to come home and unload on Emily about how difficult it was, and I had to admit to her that I wasn't really enjoying it as much as I wanted to. The whole business of trying to turn these dances around in four days was getting to me. And although my scores were respectable, and I hadn't yet found myself in the dance-off, I think the judges were beginning to see that maybe I didn't quite have the technical ability that I needed if I was going to do really well. Four or five weeks in, Bruno Tonioli made a very perceptive criticism. He could tell that I was a decent performer, he said, but I was starting to do the same things week in, week out. They needed to see more of the technical side of my dancing.

I always tried to be very respectful of the judges, even when what they had to say was critical of my performance. I came in for a bit of flak for that – there were people who seemed to think I was trying to suck up to them in order to earn myself a few brownie points. I want it known that nothing could be further from the truth. I took the view that these were not just celebrities who had been called in to judge something

because they had a famous face. They were professional dancers. If Darcey Bussell tells me my foot's in the wrong place, then my foot *is* in the wrong place. If Bruno or Len tells me I'm standing the wrong way, then I *am* standing the wrong way. They know in minute detail how every single dance is supposed to look. And it's no good lapping it up when they tell you a performance is good if, when they give you feedback you might not want to hear, you then disagree with them and say that they don't know what they're talking about. I listened to the judges, and was grateful even for their negative feedback, not because I wanted to make friends with them, but because I respected them.

'I listened to the judges, and was grateful even for their negative feedback, not because I wanted to make friends with them, but because I respected them.'

For me, it was like singing in front of a panel made up of Elton John, Rod Stewart, Michael Jackson and Prince. If they tell you you're doing something wrong, you'd better listen! So my gratitude wasn't fake: I knew they were teaching me a great deal, and I would be able to bring what I was learning from them in to my own performances in the future.

My performances on the show *were* all getting a bit samey. I felt like I was in a bit of a rut. I admitted as much to my dance partner, Janette. 'I don't know what I can do to improve,' I told her. 'I know how to perform, but I can't get my head round all this technical stuff.'

Opposite: I have the world of respect for Janette, who is the greatest dancer I have ever worked with.

Janette had a plan. She suggested that we bring on one of the really big dances. For certain routines on *Strictly*, you get the benefit of another choreographer, so you get an extra set of eyes. The Charleston was one of these, and Janette thought that it would really suit me.

She was right. Here was a dance that I could get my teeth into. I understood the rhythm and the feel, and wc had two choreographers to put us through our paces and make sure we really knew what we were doing. We were going to dance it to 'Do Your Thing' by Basement Jaxx, and I felt the same confidence going into the performance that I had going into the first show after my full three weeks of rehearsal. However, I remember saying to Emily in the days before the Charleston, 'This might be my last week.'

Opposite: By far my favourite dance, which helped us secure the highest score of the series to that point. The Charleston also gave Janette and me the first 10 from Len.

Below: I learned so much about the technical side of dancing, which I know I will use in my performances for ever.

'It was the highest-scoring dance of the series up to that point, and the reaction completely blew me away. It's no exaggeration to say that, career-wise, that was one of my greatest moments in twenty-five years.'

She gave me a strange look. 'What are you talking about?' she said. 'You're getting great marks, you're one of the top dancers.'

'Maybe,' I said. 'But if I dance this Charleston really well, I think I'll have hit my peak and I don't know if I'm going to want to carry on.'

Saturday night arrived. We went out there and we smashed it. Some people involved with the show said it was the best Charleston they'd ever seen. We received two 10s (the first of the series) and two 9s, and even Len Goodman, who had just had a knee operation, got to his feet and announced that it deserved a standing ovation.

It was the highest-scoring dance of the series up to that point, and the reaction completely blew me away. It's no exaggeration to say that, career-wise, that was one of my greatest moments in twenty-five years. I was on such a high. Rather than fill me with optimism and enthusiasm for the dances still to come, however, it had the opposite effect. I couldn't shake the feeling that the only way was down. I rang Emily and said, 'I wish someone could just break my legs now, because I don't want to do another week. I've reached my peak. Nothing's going to be as good as that.' I know it sounds bad, and I'm not usually a quitter, but I've always liked to finish on a high.

I shared my feelings with Janette. I think she found it difficult to understand where I was coming from. She tried to explain that there were some great dances coming up, like the salsa, which she thought I would be well suited to. But I knew I'd have to tackle other dances that I wouldn't be very good at. I told her that, from that point on, my only focus was to get her into the final. I didn't want it for myself. I'd had my moment, and that was the Charleston. To me, it was like doing a show at Wembley Stadium and then having to play at a succession of much smaller venues. Somehow, I just knew they wouldn't give me the same buzz.

I shared my feelings with my brother Mike. 'You're not very competitive, are you?' he said.

'Bro,' I replied, 'I'm only competitive with myself. Not with other people.'

I was setting myself up for a fall, of course.

The following week we danced the Viennese waltz to 'You're My World' by Cilla Black. I managed to hold it together and we scored a respectable two 8s and two 9s. But it was downhill from there. The following week was Blackpool Week. We were to dance the jive to 'River Deep – Mountain High' by Ike and Tina Turner.

I knew how difficult the jive was going to be. Even though it's energetic and up-tempo like the Charleston, it's a very different kind of dance. I simply couldn't feel the groove of the dance at all. I was a mess when we got to Blackpool. My brother was doing my hair. 'Oh my God,' he said, 'you've got grey hairs!'

'Bro,' I told him, 'I'm so stressed. I don't want to be doing this. I don't know all the technical things I'm supposed to. I don't know what they're talking about.'

'You'll be fine,' he assured me.

But I wasn't. I was told it wasn't a great jive. My feet were heavy. I didn't get the up-rhythm. I knew all this before the judges gave their

Our Viennese waltz to Cilla Black's
'You're My World'.

verdict and the truth was that by now I just wanted to go home. For the first time in the series, I found myself in the dance-off. I did my best, but secretly I wanted to be eliminated. I wasn't. I guess the judges thought I'd been pretty consistent up to that point, so they wanted to give me the benefit of the doubt.

I called Emily straight away. 'I'm still here,' I said. I should have been so happy about it, but I wasn't. 'I really hope I go home next week,' I told her. 'I want the technical dancers to win, not me.'

'But that's not what a competition is!' she told me.

'I know,' I said. 'But I'm not bothered about winning any more.'

I got my wish. In my final week, we danced the American smooth to 'I Get The Sweetest Feeling' by Jackie Wilson. I gave it my best shot, and our scores were respectable enough, but not sufficient to keep us in the

My final dance, and it was nothing but joy.

competition. I'd had a good run – ten weeks in all – but now it was time to go home.

I was glad that Jay McGuinness, Georgia May Foote and Kellie Bright were in the final. Jay, the winner, was a phenomenal dancer, and technically one of the best I'd ever seen. And although I doubt I'd put myself through an experience like that again, I certainly had some great moments on *Strictly*. I loved my partner Janette, and there was a great buzz backstage. The contestants were super-supportive of each other and everyone got on fantastically well. I certainly appreciate everything I learned, and I welcomed the honesty of the judges and the support of everyone who watched me. It even led to some more great TV offers, one of which came from ITV to do *Tonight at the London Palladium* for eight weeks. All in all, it was a positive experience, and I think I learned something important about myself. I'm happy just to be the best I can be. And although I could perhaps have done a lot more in the industry if I'd had that extra drive, I think that a little humility isn't such a bad thing. Maybe my lack of competitiveness is what has kept me going for so long.

One of the things I love about my manager Claire is that she always has one eye on the future. For this reason, when I'm approached to do a long-term TV project, she encourages me never to do it for more than two years. There are exceptions to this rule, of course. My reality TV projects have run and run, and if somebody turned round and offered me a regular Saturday-night entertainment spot, I would be daft not to do everything in my power to make that continue as long as possible. With other projects, however, such as TV commercials or shows where you're one of a line of presenters who have been involved, you risk being pigeonholed if you stay with them for too long. Claire's two-year rule of thumb is a very sensible one.

I'm definitely not a minute man – more like a sixty-minute man!

Having said that, I loved the TV show *Peter Andre's 60 Minute Makeover* so much that, when it had run its course, I secretly wished it could have gone on for longer. With hindsight, though, I think it was right that we stuck to the two-year rule. But I really did enjoy making that programme.

Sixty Minute Makeover had been off-air for a while when they approached me to present a new series. My first reaction was one of surprise. Why would anybody want *me* to be involved with a makeover show when I'm absolutely *hopeless* at DIY? But the programme makers explained that this was part of the fun of it. They also explained that I didn't need to worry about me and my team having to renovate a room in sixty minutes flat. At the beginning of each episode, we would explain that the makeovers are done over the course of a day, and that the viewer was about to see a sixty-minute highlight of what happened that day. Much more manageable!

> 'My first reaction was one of surprise. Why would anybody want me to be involved with a makeover show when I'm absolutely *hopeless* at DIY?'

Trust me: those days were full on. We'd start early – I'd do my intro and the guys would get stuck in to the job. Family members of the person whose home was being renovated were often in on the secret, and towards the end of the day they would have to keep the owners out of the house while we struggled to get the job done. We were often still at it at nine or ten o'clock in the evening.

Long days, but fun days. Needless to say, I was completely terrible whenever I tried to put my hand to any DIY. In fact, I'm surprised I survived. I was so clumsy, there were times I had cupboards falling on my head. They even had to make me start wearing a hard hat. Happily, everyone else on the team – the carpenters, painters and decorators, and interior designers – were very talented, all bringing their own taste and skills to the party. We became very good friends, and I often ended up having them all round to my house for a barbecue and to chill out.

But the best thing about *Peter Andre's 60 Minute Makeover* was that I genuinely feel we did some good for many people who deserved a bit of a break. Now, I'm not going to pretend that everybody was fully appreciative of what we did. One woman in particular springs to mind: when she came home, she hated what the designers had done, was very angry that people had gone behind her back to do it and entered her house without her permission. She wanted the whole thing put back to how it was before.

Other people were genuinely moved by what we'd done for them. One lady had been battling cancer and had lost her husband to the same illness. She was a teacher, which meant she was on her feet all day, and when she got home she was still busy because she had to keep the show on the road for her daughters. Those same daughters wanted to do something for their mum: to change her bedroom so that when she walked into it, she wasn't immediately confronted with all the associated memories. I'll never forget the moment she stepped into that bedroom. I'm a very emotional person and I think I felt a little bit of what she felt. I became quite overwhelmed and had to step away from the cameras while they carried on filming the family. I realized, while doing the show, that people have different needs. Some people need to win the lottery to change their lives. Some people need a new car. But for some people, simply changing the interior of one room can dramatically alter their

Sixty Minute Makeover was such a fun show to present. I think we should bring it back!

life for the better. When we revisited this lady two weeks later, she told us that she'd never felt so strong, so alive and so determined. All of a sudden, the memories in that bedroom were different. Moreover, she was truly moved that her family had wanted to do this for her.

We came across so many stories like this doing the show. There was a couple who, over the years, had fostered nearly a hundred children, with up to six kids at a time living in a house barely big enough for the two of them. There were few toys and fewer luxuries, but this couple just wanted to give food and shelter to children who needed it. We transformed a couple of rooms for them, creating an area for the kids and knowing that this would genuinely transform their lives. We met people who had suffered terrible tragedies in their family and found themselves in a rut. Their houses had fallen into disrepair, everything was broken and they couldn't afford to fix things up. We met families where the father and mother had passed away and it was up to the oldest brother to bring up his siblings with hardly any money. We met a father whose wife had died and who was doing his best to bring up their children on his own. For all these people, the simple transformation of a room in their house was actually a catalyst to solving bigger and deeper problems.

I was proud of *Peter Andre's 60 Minute Makeover*. It was enjoyable telly and fun to make, and I truly believe that it brought a good deal of happiness into the lives of some people who needed it.

Food for Thought

'What might have happened if I'd taken the Backstreet Boys up on their offer ...'

Food for Thought

I want to take you back to the mid 1990s. I was having a lot of success with my music, and I wanted to do everything I could to build on that success. And one of the things that came with success was the opportunity to work on TV commercials and product endorsements. A lot of the big names were doing it – not just musicians but sports stars and actors too.

I went to my manager Claire and asked if there was anything we could do about this. She put out some feelers and a few little bits came back. One of them was a whisper from Calvin Klein that I might be in the running to model some of their men's underwear. I'll be honest: this was something I'd always wanted to do. I admired Mark Wahlberg, who had done a series of Calvin Klein ads with the iconic photographer Herb Ritts. And though I say so myself, I was pretty ripped at the time – much more so than I am now. Calvin Klein felt like a good match for me. So we engaged a photographer and took some good shots to send in to them. I don't know whether those photos landed on the right desk or not, but nothing ever came of it.

I did a nice little campaign for Diet Coke. It was a poster campaign, and I remember those posters being everywhere for a while. I no longer have any copies of them – if anybody does, get in touch, because I'd love to see them again! All in all, however, the endorsements I managed to get were quite minor, and I didn't really know what to do about it.

I think it's important to look after yourself.
Twenty-five years later, I'm still training
hard.

'I used to go on the road with the *Smash Hits* roadshow as it travelled to all the big arenas around the country. One of my jobs every night was to introduce this virtually unknown new band called the Backstreet Boys.'

The music was going great. My singles were going to number one in the UK and I was touring all over the UK and Europe. One of my gigs was to host a show called the *Smash Hits* Poll Winners' Party. This was back when the Spice Girls were up and coming, and Ant and Dec were still PJ and Duncan – it's quite bizarre to remember a time when I was introducing them rather than them doing the introducing. I used to go on the road with the *Smash Hits* roadshow as it travelled to all the big arenas around the country. One of my jobs every night was to introduce this virtually unknown new band called the Backstreet Boys.

Every night, I'd big them up properly, telling the audience that these guys were *really* good. And I meant it. I remember the first time I saw them. They were a very cool-looking group as they piled out of their tour bus wearing big leather jackets emblazoned with their band name. My first thought was: wow, someone's investing a lot of money in these five guys. It turned out to be a wise investment.

We became very good friends. Every night I'd join them in their

Opposite: Those were the days. With Lily Savage at the *Smash Hits* Poll Winners' Party.

dressing room and we'd warm up our vocals together. We toured the roadshow through Europe together after finishing in the UK. Sometimes I'd be headlining. Imagine that – me headlining over a band who would become as massive as the Backstreet Boys.

Introducing them every night, I watched their following start to grow. You never know how success is going to affect people, but they remained lovely guys. Even as they became global superstars, we stayed in touch. Every time I saw them, it was hugs all round, and they used to open up to me now and again. I was backstage in Europe with them one time, and they all seemed kind of upset about something. I asked them what was wrong.

'It's our manager,' they said. 'He's got this other group on his books, and they perform just like us.' This band, it turned out, was *NSYNC – the band that would launch Justin Timberlake into the fame stratosphere. I tried to cheer the Backstreet Boys up.

'What are you worried about?' I asked. 'You're huge stars – so what if there's some other group. There's a million other solo singers out there, but I can't let them worry me.' But they weren't convinced, and I guess it must have been tough for them, knowing that their management was looking after two very similar acts.

Because of my association with the Backstreet Boys, I got to meet Justin Timberlake and the *NSYNC guys not long afterwards. They were just young kids then, but we got on well. I remember thinking that *NSYNC were the most incredible dancers – some of the best I'd seen – but I did genuinely think that the Backstreet Boys' vocals were better at the time. I last saw Justin Timberlake about five years ago. If I'm honest, I wasn't sure he'd remember me – he has moved on to far greater things since those days – but I was gratified by his extremely enthusiastic greeting. We had a good catch-up, reminiscing about the old days. 'Look at you now,' I said

'I last saw Justin Timberlake about five years ago. If I'm honest, I wasn't sure he'd remember me – he has moved on to far greater things since those days – but I was gratified by his extremely enthusiastic greeting.'

to him. 'You're a megastar. I could only dream of hitting the heights you've managed. You're an incredible talent.' And it's true. My old friend is at the top. He manages to appeal to everybody. His music is not too cheesy, not too urban, he's charming, he's a great actor. He's got it just right.

Back in the day, though, the arrival of *NSYNC on the scene was the first time I noticed a little bit of dissatisfaction on the part of the Backstreet Boys towards their manager, Lou Pearlman. I don't have many regrets in my life, but one of them is that I didn't take that dissatisfaction a bit more seriously.

Cut to the end of the 1990s. I was in LA – I've told you how much I like LA, right? My first album had gone to number one in the UK, and I'd just finished recording my *Time* album, on which I'd worked with great artists like Brian McKnight – for my money one of the best soul singers of our generation – Warren G, Coolio, the Fugees and Montell Jordan. One day I found myself in the same hotel as Lou Pearlman. I decided I had to go and see him, since we knew each other from the days when I was hanging out with the Backstreet Boys and *NSYNC. I wasn't quite sure what reception I was going to get, but I knocked on his hotel door anyway.

Lou appeared in his boxer shorts. He couldn't have been more

On my *Natural* tour in 1997. Things were going from strength to strength with my music, as I'd just secured a number-one album.

welcoming (not in that way, you cheeky lot!). 'Dude, come on in! I'm just getting dressed ...' I sat down and waited for him. When he joined me, fully dressed now, he had a very interesting proposition. 'You need to sign up with me,' he said. 'I can help you break America. You're wasting too much time sitting it out in England ...'

'But I've got this massive fan base in England,' I said.

'Sure,' Lou replied, 'and we'll keep that. But I can make you huge in America. So what do you say? Do you want me to manage you?'

For any performing artist, breaking America is the holy grail. I'd never even performed there, so I was very tempted by Lou's offer. I was also very loyal to my manager Claire – as I write this, we've been together for twenty-two years – and I wasn't going to turn my back on her after

everything she'd done for me. So I put my cards on the table. 'Do you mind if I experiment with America for a couple of years?' I asked her. 'I won't neglect my fan base in England, but it seems to me that I've got an opportunity here.'

Claire wasn't going to stand in my way. She didn't think it was an especially good idea, but she supported me when she realized this was something I really wanted to do. And so I made the decision to sign with Lou Pearlman.

One night, not so long afterwards, I bumped into Kevin Richardson from the Backstreet Boys. 'Listen,' I told him, 'I've decided to sign up with Lou. He's going to help me break America.'

I guess I expected him to be as excited about this as me. I was a bit taken aback when he wasn't. 'Don't do it,' he said.

'Why not?' I asked him.

'Come with us instead,' Kevin urged me. By this time the Backstreet Boys were absolutely colossal and they had their own record label. 'Sign to us, you can come on tour with us and *we'll* make you big in America.'

So now I had two great offers, and I was conflicted. I tried to explain to him that I was committed to Lou and that he seemed a really nice guy. No matter what I said, Kevin kept trying to persuade me. In the end, however, I decided that I had to honour my original commitment to Lou. Your word counts for a lot in this industry, and I wanted to keep mine.

Fair play to Lou: he started the ball rolling in America and I found myself in negotiations with all the big names – Coke, Pepsi, McDonald's – with which you need to be associated if you want the best chance of cracking America. The people who mattered were on board. All they needed was the green light from Lou to say that a new album was ready to go so that my endorsements could be coordinated with my material being released in the American market. It never happened. Lou

On my 1996 arena tour. Maybe the Judge Dredd look was a bit over the top.

and I remained friends, but my storming of America didn't materialize. Years later, Lou would be sentenced to twenty-five years in federal prison for fraud. There was talk of further disagreements with some of the bands he managed. Even though I never fell out with Lou, perhaps I was best out of it. I returned to the UK and and have concentrated on outside of America ever since. What might have happened if I'd taken the Backstreet Boys up on their offer still gives me food for thought ...

Success continued in the UK. I carried on recording albums and touring extensively. I soon forgot about Lou Pearlman and what might have been. I never forgot about endorsements, though, and particularly TV commercials. It seems a little ironic to me that it took a couple of decades for them to start coming through, but hey, better late than never! I was in my late thirties when the offer landed on Claire's desk for me to be the face of the Iceland brand.

When Iceland first approached me, I was in two minds about whether or not to get involved. I'd seen some previous Iceland commercials and they didn't seem to be quite my thing. It's important to keep an open mind in this business, however, so when Iceland invited me up to their head office to talk to them about the project, I accepted.

Food is very important to me. In fact, I'd go further than that. After my family, food is my life. I've always joked that we might not be perfect as human beings, but the bit of us that gets closest to perfection is our tastebuds. If somebody offered you a world where there was no violence and where nobody gets sick or grows old, you'd be there in a second. If somebody offered you a world where food tastes really great, you wouldn't be so fussed because the food here *already* tastes amazing! It's one of life's greatest pleasures and I've always felt blessed that I enjoy it so much, because it's a source of such joy for me. I love cooking more than ever at the moment, and I love thinking about it too.

I grew up in a big Greek family, and in Greek families food is a big deal. Put it this way: at traditional Cypriot weddings, two thousand people turn up. They block off sections of the village and everyone in the intervening streets is invited. For us, food is not just nutrition, it's the centre of our social world, a way of life.

I'm grateful that, when we were growing up on the Gold Coast, my mum and dad took great care to make sure we were fed healthy food. Not that I always appreciated it at the time. Monday nights usually involved boiled black-eyed peas with spinach, olive oil and lemon. That was my worst nightmare and the reason why Monday was my worst day of the week – I had to go to school *and* I had to eat boiled black-eyed peas. Tuesdays were even worse – lentils, probably. I hated lentils even more than I hated black-eyed peas. Wednesday would be another vegetarian option, and things only really started to look up on Thursday, when we'd have something like lamb chops and chips. So Thursdays were really exciting, and things became even better on Friday night, which was pasta night in the Andréa household. At the weekend it was the typical Greek food that we all loved. So when I look back on my upbringing, I realize that my parents were doing their best to ensure that we didn't just have a heavily meat-based diet. I hated all the beans, spinach and pumpkin at the time, but I'm grateful for my mum and dad's watchful parenting now.

When I started living on my own, all that healthy eating went out of the window. I turned a bit crazy when it came to food and started eating all the unhealthy foods I wasn't allowed to eat as a kid. Fortunately, I was training very hard because I knew I needed to keep in shape to maximize my chances of success in the profession that I had chosen. In the entertainment industry, they say it matters what you look like. I was lucky that I had the discipline to keep exercising – without that I could have easily ballooned on the back of the kind of food I was eating. You see it happen a lot with footballers and other sportsmen when they retire. They've been so strict for so long that they rebel when they hang up their boots. And while on the one hand it's good to be in an industry that demands you look after yourself, on the other hand it's not so great because you can be very self-conscious on those occasions when you want to let yourself go a little ...

Nowadays I eat pretty much what I desire but I have to continue my training in order to keep trim. It's made even harder by the fact that I have a stunning wife who manages to maintain a six-pack without doing anything at all.

'Nowadays I eat pretty much what I desire but I have to continue my training in order to keep trim. It's made even harder by the fact that I have a stunning wife who manages to maintain a six-pack without doing anything at all.'

Emily has really changed the way I think about food. Before I met her, I couldn't imagine not having a big dinner every single night. Anything else was alien to me because that was all I'd ever known. It came as a surprise when she sometimes said she wasn't that hungry of an evening and only fancied a sandwich. But her outlook has helped me think even more carefully about the food that I eat.

So, when I visited the Iceland head office, they showed me round all the different departments they had. I was amazed. I had always

It was great to help with the change of Iceland's marketing strategy, to show people the power of frozen. They were brilliant to work with.

associated the brand with – I'll be honest – frozen party food, but now I saw that as well as their big frozen and tinned departments they sold lots of fresh food, frozen at source. They were clearly a company that dealt with good, healthy products. Given my enthusiasm for proper food, my interest was piqued.

'Why don't you advertise all this?' I asked them. 'All I ever see you marketing is your frozen food.'

They explained to me that this strategy was dictated by the market but that they hoped, over time and with my help, to change the brand so that people would begin to understand that there was more to Iceland than they had previously thought.

This felt like something I could enjoy doing. I wanted to be honest with myself, and only endorse products I felt good about. I explained to them that I didn't really want to be seen advertising the kinds of foods I'd seen Iceland marketing before. Their response was that they needed to start where they had left off but they would avoid the party foods. As time went on, they would gradually move to advertising more of the products that I was interested in.

Iceland were as good as their word. To start off with, we advertised frozen vegetables and other products that I would happily feed my children. As the campaign continued, we moved on to more interesting foods – fresh salmon frozen at source, king prawns, lobsters. There were some great products, and Emily and I genuinely became converts. It was great to be part of what I thought of as a little food revolution. We were trying to show people that, in many instances, buying frozen food could actually be better than buying fresh food. What often happens is that people buy fresh food from the supermarket, then go home and put it in the freezer. The products I was advertising at Iceland, however, had often been frozen much more quickly – peas picked fresh and frozen within ninety minutes, salmon or prawns caught and frozen at source. This is much healthier and — weirdly — 'fresher' than doing it the other way.

I knew that, at first, I was going to get a bit of flak for taking these commercials on. Sometimes, though, you've just got to go with your gut feeling and actually people did start to enjoy the commercials because they were, I think, very funny. The conceit was that I would be doing my shopping in Iceland and, seeing me, people would come up and say: 'Oh my God, I can't believe it!' I would be blind to the fact that they were referring to me, and would think they were talking about the price of the frozen peas, or whatever we were advertising. It was a simple gag, but effective. A great little campaign.

My deal with Iceland was such that we would do a year's worth of commercials and then, if they were successful, extend for another year. As I've already mentioned, two years is a good period of time to be doing

I do love to cook! Here I am doing an impromptu cooking demonstration in Leeds to promote Iceland's frozen range. I knocked up some amazing sea bass, then gave the passers-by some of my Aussie barbecue tips!

something like this. From a professional point of view, it was probably the most lucrative job I've ever had – bigger in that respect than any sell-out tours I've ever done, strange though it may sound. A life-changing deal. But more than that, it was a lot of fun. I got to work with some truly lovely people on a project that I was enthusiastic about.

As you can probably tell, I have fond feelings towards my time working with Iceland. You can tell a lot about a company, I think, by meeting the people who run it. The boss of Iceland – Malcolm Walker – was always very nice to me. (It was a memorable day when he picked me up in his helicopter and took me into London. The journey that normally takes two hours by car took us four and a half minutes.) You can tell even more by how they treat others: Iceland has raised many millions of pounds for great causes such as the Alder Hey Children's Hospital, Help for Heroes and Alzheimer's Research. They also helped me raise tens of thousands of pounds for the Cancer Research UK Peter Andre Fund. I'm proud to be associated with them for that reason alone. The Iceland deal opened up a host of other fantastic food-related opportunities for me. Tesco now stock my own brand of coffee and I'm developing a range of olive oils, marinades, cheeses and wines. Look out for them on a supermarket shelf near you soon!

I liked working with Iceland so much, I even released an exclusive album for them. I wanted, just for a bit of fun, to do an Elvis-style Christmas album. It was called *White Christmas*, and on it I sang in a much lower register than I ever had before. Some fans weren't too sure about it, but it appealed to a lot of people who'd never heard me sing before. As a result, I've had a lot of requests to produce more material of me singing in that register. That's unlikely to happen – it was really just a bit of an experiment – but the record sold out at Iceland. You could say it was the icing on the frozen cake.

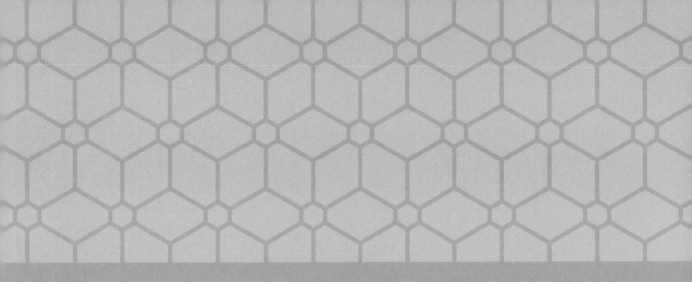

The Business

'The only ones who don't succeed
are the ones who quit.'

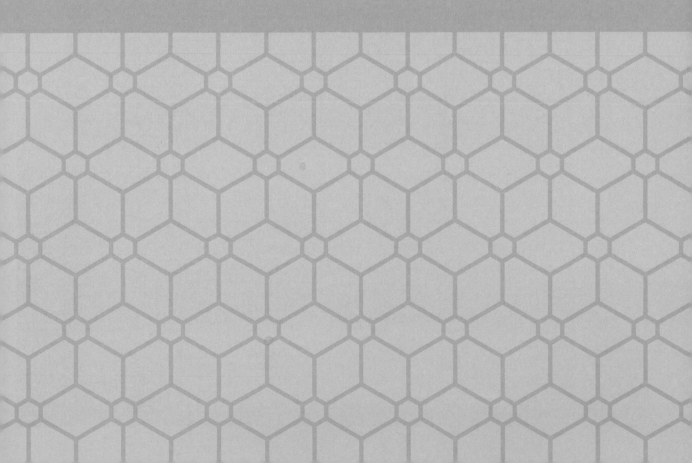

The Business

Longevity is very difficult to achieve in this business. I've seen a lot of people come and go. Just the other day I saw a poster advertising an event which I'm headlining. The support acts are all people who were way bigger than me back in the day, and are now lower down on the bill. For anyone – me included – who thinks it's a given that they'll stay top of the pile in the music game, that's a sobering thought.

There's an old saying: be nice to people on the way up, because the chances are you'll see them on the way down too. One of the reasons I think I'm still standing after more than twenty-five years in the industry is that I always try to treat people with the proper respect. This is partly because of the values instilled in me by my mum and dad when I was growing up, and partly because I received the same treatment when I first came to the UK.

The band East 17 had come to Australia some time previously and we did a dual-headlining tour. The boys and I hit it off really well and when the tour was over, I said to Brian Harvey, 'If I ever come to England, would you let me open for your tour?'

Brian was unequivocal. 'I give you my word,' he said. 'If you ever come to the UK, I'll let you be our support act.' He was as good as his word, despite some others in the East 17 camp being reluctant to let me join them. A lot of people don't realize that a support act has to pay to share the bill on a tour with a major act. When I thanked one person associated with East 17 for letting me join them, they just shrugged and said, 'Your money's as green as anyone else's.' It was a reminder that not everyone in the industry is as supportive and respectful as Brian and the rest of the band members were. That tour with East 17 really kickstarted my fan base. I'll be forever grateful to them for giving me that opportunity, and I'm sad to think that they're not so big any more. They know, however, that they can always call on me to help them out in whatever way I can. That's the way it works.

'One of the reasons I think I'm still standing after more than twenty-five years in the industry is that I always try to treat people with the proper respect.'

I was once performing at the MTV Europe Music Awards. I was sitting in my dressing room with my brother Danny and there was a knock at the door. It was Robbie Williams. This was after he'd left Take That, but before he'd made it big as a solo artist. 'Can I come and share your dressing room with you?' he asked. It turned out that someone else on the bill – I'm not going to name names! – had kicked Robbie out of his dressing room because he was a 'bigger' act. Soon enough, of course, Robbie was a megastar. This other artist? Not so much. Another reminder that fame is fickle and nobody in our industry ever really knows what the future holds.

I've always been of the opinion that it's important to be a bit of a Jack of all trades if longevity in the entertainment industry is your aim. That's why I've found myself doing all sorts of things, from TV presenting to movie cameos to charity events to public speaking. And I'm lucky enough to have in Claire a manager who can think outside the box and come up with great ideas, but also take my ideas and run with them.

One of the first jobs I ever had as a kid was selling men's fragrances at a department store. Years later, that gave me the idea of releasing my own men's fragrance. I spoke to Claire about this, and she organized a massive amount of research. We learned that most fragrances – even men's fragrances – are bought by women. When women were asked whether they would prefer a Peter Andre men's fragrance or a Peter Andre women's fragrance, their response was overwhelmingly on the side of the women's fragrance.

Incredibly, we have just released our ninth ladies' fragrance, which is going from strength to strength.

As with everything else I do, I'm very closely involved with my fragrance line, from the artwork to the design of the bottles and, of course, to the scent itself. I'm forever testing new scents on my wife, my mum, my sister and basically most of the women I know! I'm very diligent about putting out a product that I myself would want to buy for someone. It's taken a little time to get it right. We've had to learn about technical things such as the alcohol content of a perfume – if it's too high the scent can be overpowering, if it's too low it wears off very quickly. And while the first couple of fragrances we produced didn't sell all that well, by the time we got on to our third, people were buying it at a rate of one bottle every thirty seconds. It's taken time, but we've really built the line into something I'm immensely proud of.

I'm involved in everything from the scent itself to the bottle design.

With the future in mind, however, I've always known that it would be sensible to have other interests outside of the industry. That way, if the time comes when I can no longer sustain an entertainment career, I've got something to fall back on. And with food being so important to me, I guess it's no surprise that I've found myself diversifying into that area.

Fifteen years ago, I was in New York with my brothers Michael and Danny. During that trip, we went to one of the early Starbucks outlets. It was very cool. People were hanging out, working at their laptops or reading books. I'd only recently seen the movie *You've Got Mail* with Tom Hanks and Meg Ryan, which I'd loved, and that coffee shop seemed to capture something of the movie's vibe. I'm a bit of a coffee fanatic, and I remember saying to my brothers: one day, I'm going to own a place like this.

'With food being so important to me, I guess it's no surprise that I've found myself diversifying into that area.'

The idea came up again years later, in around 2012. Truth to tell it never really went away. Having grown up in Australia, where the coffee culture is really strong and where it's almost impossible to get a bad cup of coffee, I couldn't quite understand why it was difficult to get a good one in the UK – despite the number of high street coffee chains that were popping up all over the place. I suggested to Danny that we just go ahead and set up our own coffee shop.

I'm primarily a performer rather than a businessman. But I'm lucky, because my dad is very business-minded. I've learned so much from him, and from the way he's made businesses work in the past. He is a barber by trade – he still owns a barber shop in Paddington, despite living in Australia. When we first moved to the Gold Coast, he didn't want to continue in the barber business, though. One day he was chatting with an architect friend of his who showed him some plans he'd made for a house. Dad made a couple of suggestions as to how the house could be improved, which the architect loved. 'You should get into this,' he told my dad, who took him at his word. Dad became one of the first to build luxury residential homes on the Gold Coast. His friend who started making developments with him went on to build some of the biggest, grandest buildings in Australia, but Dad never wanted to do that. 'The bigger you build them,' he told me, 'the harder they're going to fall.' So he stuck to the residential houses, but made a great success of his business. He has that kind of mind.

My mum, too, is a real clever clogs. She understands how to build a business portfolio and between them, they're quite a team. I call them nearly every day and ask them for their advice. I pretty much couldn't do my business without them, and they're instrumental to our family coffee outfit.

To start with, we thought of our coffee shop as little more than somewhere we ourselves could go to have good coffee. But the idea soon started to grow. It was Mike's idea to call it the New York Coffee Club. I'd first had the idea in New York, after all, and if I were to start up enough of these places, it would be like a little club. I could do a Greenwich Village-style outlet, a SoHo-style outlet, a Little Italy-style outlet. I was beginning to warm to the idea.

From the outset, I was determined that if I were to start a coffee shop, it should have a play area for children. I used to take my kids to Starbucks on a Saturday morning when they were much smaller. They'd be all excited on Friday night because they knew they were going to get a treat the following morning. But when they actually got there, they were bored out of their brains within ten minutes and would want to leave.

I, on the other hand, would want to stay and deal with my emails or read the paper. For that reason, I came up with the concept of a children's area where the kids would be occupied and could have fun while their parents relaxed and enjoyed their coffee. I felt sure that it would win people over.

Typical me: I didn't want to do anything by halves. Instead of going out there and getting another investor to come in and share the financial load with me, I decided I was going to pay for everything. I'm not going to deny that it was very costly, but that was how I wanted it to be done. My brother Danny, who was to be the coffee shop manager, was very involved too once we found some great premises in East Grinstead, very close to where I live. As the project went ahead, Danny especially helped with the decor, picking out the colours while we got builders in to fit the place out exactly how we wanted it – and of course, to install the all-important children's play area.

The launch of the coffee shop was absolutely crazy. Thousands of people congregated outside, there was a media scrum and the whole day was absolutely manic. We knew, however, that once the initial kerfuffle had died down, the coffee shop itself would have to stand on its own merits. I was confident that the children's area would win people over, and so it did. Some mornings, and some afternoons after school, you can't even walk into the place for all the buggies! Mums and dads love that their kids can use the play area while they relax and chat.

Even more important than that, however, was that the coffee itself should be good. Because the coffee's the most important thing in a coffee shop, right? From the outset, we wanted to serve the kind of coffee we enjoyed in Australia. In other words: coffee that is not bitter and which doesn't need any sugar to make it palatable. The milk should never be burned, and the blend should be just right. We developed two different

Launching New York Coffee Club was something I've always wanted to do. We have a little kids' play area so parents can sit and enjoy the best flat whites this side of Manhattan.

blends – a stronger one for the milky coffee, and a smoother one for the espresso shots. (Did I mention that I was passionate about coffee?!)

Our attention to detail with respect to the coffee has paid off. Reviews regularly state that we serve the best coffee people have tasted, and that's exactly what I wanted to achieve when we first set out on this path. As a result of that, the shop in East Grinstead has been a massive success. We have a loyal following and our product is spot on. With a hit on our hands, I thought it might make sense to open a second shop. We decided on Brighton – which was not too far away – for the location.

A lot of people thought I was doing too much too soon. Why rush to open a Brighton shop when I'd only just got the East Grinstead one up and running? Well, I had grand plans for my coffee business, and I wanted to have two on the go to convince myself that the idea would work if I tried to expand it. We went ahead and opened up this enormous shop in Brighton. I couldn't purchase these particular premises, so I agreed to

At the opening of the New York Coffee Club – a real family affair.

rent them. The rent was sky high, but I decided to give it a go for three years and, if it was successful, re-evaluate at the end of that time.

We ran the Brighton shop for the three years and it was fantastic. People loved the coffee shop and I was very proud of it. When the three years were up, however, we had a call to make. The truth was that we were giving practically all our profit away in rent. It didn't matter how busy we were. We could be selling coffee from first thing in the morning till last thing at night and we would still only just be breaking even. So when the lease expired, I decided to take things in a different direction. I met a lady whose company was involved with massive outdoor events and festivals. She approached us with the idea of building big mobile coffee units with our brand that we could take to festivals.

I liked the idea very much. Reluctantly I closed the Brighton shop and invested in one of these coffee units. As I write this, we have three units in total which we've taken to all sorts of events — V Festival, Wireless, the Proms — and which have proved to be enormously successful. My aim is to own twenty of these units by the time I'm fifty. I've kept the shop in East Grinstead, however. It's doing great (for the third year running it's been awarded top marks — five stars — for its food hygiene rating by the FSA) and we have loads of wonderful customers — plus, it's a fantastic place for me to nip down to when I fancy a decent coffee! I'm always happy to chat to fans if I meet them there, and sometimes you'll even find me behind the counter, helping out my brother and our brilliant staff.

I'm considering changing the name of our brand from the New York Coffee Club to Andre's. Lots of people suggested that I did that at the beginning. I was reluctant, though. The way I saw it, the brand had to stand on its own if it was going to be successful in the long term, without having to rely on a name people already knew. However, now that I've seen that it is successful, I'd consider using our family name. It is, after

Did I mention I
love my coffee?

all, very much a family business, and one that we'd like to expand even further. Chris and I also have the idea of doing a Greek taverna, but it doesn't have to stop there. The possibilities are endless. Andre's pizzas, Andre's jacket potatoes, Andre's deli. So all I can say is, watch this space …

TV work. Commercials. Coffee shops. Fragrance lines. Restaurants. Charity work. Public speaking. These are all very important parts of my professional life. But my real business is music. It always has and always will be my first love. I came into the entertainment industry because I wanted to be a musical performer, and everything else I do is in the service of that aim.

The *Revelation* album, which I'd funded myself back before I met Emily, had been a massive hit for me. The label that released it wanted a follow-up. This became the *Accelerate* album. It had a bit more of a club-like, urban feel to it — more thumping, four-to-the-floor beats. Although there were some songs on it that I really loved, there were a few I wasn't so sure about. In the end I lost a bit of control over the album, and it wasn't as commercially successful as *Revelation* had been. On the other hand, it was an interesting experiment which produced some material that went down fantastically well performed live.

I had a lot more creative freedom on my next record, *Angels and Demons*. I really loved making that album, and had the chance to work with some great artists and a lot of up-and-coming songwriters. I wanted to take the urban sound a bit further, even more so than on *Accelerate*. That album was more commercially successful than its predecessor — it just missed out on hitting the top ten — and again it produced a lot of material that went down really well at my live shows.

In 2014, my musical output took a very different direction. The album *Big Night* was my first venture into swing and blues. I got together with a great new songwriter called Stevie Appleton. He's extremely talented and I liked him the moment I met him. A lot of swing albums contain cover versions of the classics but we decided that we wanted to make an album full of completely original material for ours.. This was a big, bold move. My biggest-selling album of recent years had been *Revelation*, and this was a complete change. Sometimes, though, you've just got to go with your gut. I'd grown up listening to swing music alongside the pop and funk that I love so much, so in my head it wasn't such a big jump.

I loved that record, and it was as we were preparing it that a call came in from DreamWorks. They were releasing a movie called *Mr Peabody & Sherman*, and they wanted to meet with me to discuss a possible collaboration. A call from a major Hollywood studio is not something you ignore, so I was very excited to go and meet them in London. They asked if I would consider writing the official song for the UK release of the movie.

What an honour to have co-written and recorded the official UK song for the number-one smash-hit DreamWorks movie *Mr Peabody & Sherman*.

As it happened, Stevie Appleton had recently come up with a song that was intended for the *Big Night* album. It was called 'C'mon' and I thought it would be perfect — a bright, upbeat, rock 'n' roll pop song. Sure, we'd have to change it a little, but when I played it to DreamWorks, they loved it. Stevie and I rewrote it together and changed the title: the song 'Kid' was born. It got the green light from DreamWorks in the US, and before I knew it I had the official song to a number-one box-office smash. I was very happy that it ended up being on albums all over the world. And it was kind of ironic that the first time anyone heard me sing in America was not with 'Mysterious Girl', the song with which I'm mainly associated, but with 'Kid', a song I didn't record until two decades into my career. That's how it is in my job — you never know what's round the corner.

> 'It was kind of ironic that the first time anyone heard me sing in America was not with 'Mysterious Girl', the song with which I'm mainly associated, but with 'Kid', a song I didn't record until two decades into my career.'

The album *Big Night* didn't chart all that well — it just missed out on a top twenty spot — but I was very pleased with my first foray into recording predominantly with live musicians rather than with samples, as I had done in the past. Moreover, it was brilliant for touring. Audiences loved those tunes, and I found that although the project may not have sold many records, I sold a lot of concert tickets on the back of it. And as I've always said: as long as I'm selling tickets, I ain't quitting nothing!

Big Night also caught the attention of Warner Music. I'd worked with Warner before, and knew them to be a great label. But I was surprised when they approached me again to say that they really liked this new swing direction I had taken. They explained that 2015 was the centenary of Frank Sinatra's birth and they wanted a project to pay homage to him, with an album of all the famous swing tunes. They had Michael Bublé on the label but he wasn't releasing anything that year. Would I be interested?

This was a scary prospect for me. I had to think about who I'd be compared to. Michael Bublé's known for the swing stuff, Robbie Williams had successfully tackled the Rat Pack stuff, and then of course you've got the originals, the Frank Sinatras and Dean Martins, whom no one can even come close to. So many people had recorded these songs so brilliantly. Why would anybody want to hear my versions? Surely I'd just attract criticism for even trying? I asked my parents and my brothers for their advice, but in the end Warner knew how to persuade me. They dangled the bait of a thirty-piece big band to back me up. Once I heard that, I knew I had to take the project on, if only for the experience. If nothing else, I'd have a record of myself with all these awesome musicians – the horn section, the drums, the bass, the percussion – for my own pleasure.

I made the decision early on that I didn't want to try to be too clever with what would become the *Come Fly With Me* album. These were classic songs, and I didn't see any benefit in trying to make them more my style. I wanted to tip my hat to the greats, to be as respectful and as authentic as possible. Because let's be honest: nobody's ever going to record these songs better than Frank Sinatra and Dean Martin.

This was a big-budget album, and I was knocked out by the authenticity of the whole project – the fantastic arrangements, the instrumentations, the big fat horn section! When I put this album alongside my earlier records, there's really no comparison in terms of production values. I really loved making it, and it seemed that the public were on the same page, as it reached the number-three spot in the UK album chart. After everything I've told you about the difficulty of maintaining longevity in this business, I was thrilled and a little bit amazed to have my tenth solo album reach such heights.

So now, as I finish writing this book, I find myself in talks with Warner once again to do a follow-up swing album. In many ways I feel like this is a crossroads in my musical life. My first love, musically, is funk and soul. I had always intended, once the *Come Fly With Me* album was released, to throw myself into that musical genre. But I'm not in the position of someone like George Michael, who has sold tens of millions of albums and can pretty much dictate what kind of album he is going to record. Back in 2008, when I was making my *Revelation* album, I paid for the whole record myself. It was a big risk, but this was music that I truly wanted to make, and thankfully it paid off: once the record was in the can, a deal was struck with the label

Twenty years after my number-one album, it's great to be on the cover of *Music Week* with another top-three UK album.

Being on stage is what I love doing most. Check out the belt – Elvis would have been proud of that.

who paid me back what I'd spent on it, and *Revelation* went almost double platinum. I know that I might have to do something similar with the funk/soul album I have in mind. On the other hand, the backing of a major label to record a second swing album is not something I can easily turn down. Plus, it was an awesome experience which led to a recording that very many people seemed to enjoy. So I have a choice to make: funk/soul or swing. As dilemmas go, it's a pretty sweet one, and above all I'm grateful to be in a position where I have these choices to make. Again: watch this space ...

I've come up with a saying: 'The only ones who don't succeed are the ones who quit.' I truly believe that. My business is like being in a boxing ring. If you get knocked down, you've got to stand up again. You lose your title, you've got to win it back. I've experienced plenty of ups and downs in my career. One of the main reasons I'm still going is because I know that every time I experience a setback, I need to dust myself down and look to the future.

What's true in my professional life is also true in my personal life. The past five years have been a rollercoaster for me. I experienced some of the most terrible times I have ever known when I lost my brother Andrew, but also some of the happiest as my relationship with Emily blossomed and a new child arrived in our lives. And of course, through all of this, I have had my other beautiful children by my side. I look to the future knowing that my world will never be the same, for wonderful reasons as well as sad ones. I also know that, if the past is a good guide, the future will be anything but predictable!

Emily and I have never made any secret of the fact that we'd like to expand the family, and as I write these words I'm thrilled to say that we have another child on the way. To keep things unpredictable, I'm not going to find out whether we're having a boy or a girl in advance. I don't think this will be our last child, but I've never had the experience of not finding out the sex beforehand, so that will be a great thing for us both to experience. Well, I'm going to *try* not to find out the sex – I know what I'm like! The kids are just as excited as Emily and me. We're already getting them involved by asking them to come up with names for their new brother or sister. The other day, when we were all in the car together, I said to them, 'Do you realize that now, at this moment, there's already a family of six in the car?'

I'd like that family to increase in size even further. I've decided I don't want to be changing nappies at the age of fifty, but I'm only forty-three now so we've still got time to have another child – or three!

Whatever the future has in store, I remain grateful for the family and loved ones who surround me, and the incredible support of all those fans who have helped me sustain a career I love for more than twenty-five years. It's been quite a ride, but I've lost no enthusiasm for the journey. So here's to the next twenty-five!

Words can't describe how much I love this boy.

Picture Credits

CAN = courtesy CAN Management Ltd; CRUK = courtesy Cancer Research UK; DK = courtesy Dan Kennedy; PA = courtesy Peter Andre.

2–3: DK; 6–7: (*top row, left to right*) PA, CAN, PA, CAN, PA, CAN; (*second row, left to right*) CAN, PA, PA, CAN, CAN, CAN; (*third row, left to right*) PA, CAN, CAN, CAN, CAN; (*bottom row, left to right*) PA, PA, PA, CAN, PA; 8: DK; 10: Getty Images; 13: © WENN Ltd/Alamy Stock Photo; 14: CAN; 16: CAN; 17: CAN; 18: all images CAN; 22–3: DK; 27: Getty Images; 28–9: Getty Images; 32: CAN; 37: PA; 40: © WENN Ltd/Alamy Stock Photo; 43: Getty Images; 45: CAN; 47: CAN; 49: all images CAN; 50: CAN; 53: PA; 55: PA; 57: PA; 59: PA; 60: CAN; 62–3: CAN; 64: (*clockwise from top left*) Getty Images, PA, CAN, CAN, CAN; 67: all images CAN; 70: Getty Images; 74: all images PA; 77: CAN; 82–3: DK; 85: PA; 87: © WENN Ltd/Alamy Stock Photo; 90: Getty Images; 94: CAN; 100–1: DK; 106: all images CRUK; 107: CRUK; 109: CRUK; 110: CRUK; 111: CRUK; 112–13: CAN; 115: CAN; 116: CAN; 118: CAN; 119: all images CAN; 120: CAN; 121: CAN; 123: CAN; 125: CAN; 126: CAN; 129: CAN; 130: CAN; 135: PA; 140: CAN; 142: all images CAN; 143: CAN; 145: CAN; 148: CAN; 151: all images CAN; 152: CAN; 153: all images CAN; 154: CAN; 155: CAN; 157: CAN; 158: all images CAN; 160: all images CAN; 161: CAN; 162: © WENN Ltd/Alamy Stock Photo; 167: CAN; 169: CAN; 173: all images CAN; 174: DK; 175: DK; 179: Georgie Gillard/Associated Newspapers/REX/Shutterstock; 181: Getty Images; 183: Getty Images; 184: Jonathan Hordle/REX/Shutterstock; 186: CAN; 191: CAN; 193: CAN; 196: CAN; 198: CAN; 200: copyright © BBC Photo Library; 201: copyright © BBC Photo Library; 204–5: copyright © BBC Photo Library; 206: copyright © BBC Photo Library; 208: ITV/REX/Shutterstock; 211: CAN; 212: Getty Images; 215: Getty Images; 217: David Cheskin/PA Archive/Press Association Images; 220: CAN; 221: CAN; 222: Getty Images; 226: CAN; 228: © WENN Ltd/Alamy Stock Photo; 230: Getty Images; 234: CAN; 235: Getty Images; 239: Getty Images; 240–1: Getty Images; 242: Getty Images; 243: (*left*) John Connor Press Assocs Ltd/REX/Shutterstock, (*right*) CAN; 245: Getty Images; 247: Getty Images; 250: CAN; 251: CAN; 253: PA; 256: DK.

Acknowledgements

I've always made it clear that family is number one for me. My beautiful wife, Emily, and my adorable children are everything I live for now. I feel so lucky to have a huge family of wonderful people without whom I quite simply cannot function. My incredibly selfless mother and father, Thea and Savva, along with my brothers Andrew, Chris, Danny and Michael, and my sister, Debbie. The last few years have been tricky for us as a family, due to losing our eldest brother to cancer. We have mourned and suffered, and there have been many dark days since that tragedy. However, an incredibly tight bond has grown between all of us. Unbreakable, in fact. We are so appreciative for all we have, and I honestly mean it when I say I am humbled by the love and support from the public.

I would like to give a big thank you to Claire Powell, my friend and manager for over twenty years, and to her team who have experienced much of this with me, and continue to do so.

Huge thanks to Adam Parfitt, who patiently sat with me through the whole process of writing this book. Also to Michelle Signore, Rebecca Wright, Graeme Andrew and the team at Transworld for all the hard work they've put into this book.

To find out more about Cancer Research UK's Peter Andre Fund
and how you can get involved to help improve early cancer diagnosis
please visit: www.cruk.org/paf or www.cruk.org/peteschamps
email: peterandrefund@cancer.org.uk
call: 0203 469 5588

www.newyorkcoffeeclub.co.uk